Implementing Cloud Design Patterns for AWS

Create highly efficient design patterns for scalability, redundancy, and high availability in the AWS Cloud

Marcus Young

BIRMINGHAM - MUMBAI

Implementing Cloud Design Patterns for AWS

First published: April 2015

Production reference: 1240415

Published by Packt Publishing Ltd.
Livery Place
35 Livery Street
Birmingham B3 2PB, UK.

ISBN 978-1-78217-734-0

www.packtpub.com

Credits

Author
Marcus Young

Reviewers
João Ferreira Loff
Robert M. Marks
Somanath Nanda
Philip O'Toole
Fred Stluka

Commissioning Editor
Dipika Gaonkar

Acquisition Editor
Nikhil Karkal

Content Development Editor
Merwyn D'souza

Technical Editor
Mitali Somaiya

Copy Editors
Trishya Hajare
Sonia Mathur
Alpha Singh

Project Coordinator
Neha Bhatnagar

Proofreaders
Joanna McMahon
Paul Hindle

Indexer
Mariammal Chettiyar

Graphics
Abhinash Sahu

Production Coordinator
Aparna Bhagat

Cover Work
Aparna Bhagat

About the Author

Marcus Young recently graduated with a degree in computer science and mathematics before getting involved in system administration and DevOps. He currently works in software automation using open source tools and technologies. His hobbies include playing ice hockey and brewing homebrew beer. He also enjoys hardware projects based on microcontrollers and single board computers.

I'd like to thank my beautiful wife for putting up with the many projects and work items that make their way into my free time. Also to my son who continues to inspire me to keep pushing myself.

About the Reviewers

João Ferreira Loff has an MSc in Computer Science and Engineering with a major in software engineering from Instituto Superior Técnico (`www.tecnico.ulisboa.pt`), University of Lisboa, Portugal. His interest in Cloud computing emerged from his master's thesis, where he researched predictive elasticity for Cloud applications.

He currently collaborates with the Distributed Systems Group at INESC-ID Lisboa (`www.inesc-id.pt`), a nonprofit computer science and electronics research institute, where he researches the latest developments in Cloud computing provisioning, elasticity, and scalability.

As a part of his research he developed Vadara, a generic Cloud computing elasticity framework that allows for the development of elasticity strategies that are decoupled from Cloud providers (`https://github.com/jfloff/vadara`). The foundation of this framework has been the subject of a published work at a top tier Cloud computing conference.

You can read more about him at `https://jfloff.github.io`.

Robert M. Marks is an experienced software developer and has spent over 12 years of his career working for a variety of software companies, ranging from large companies, such as IBM, to small start-ups. He is passionate about crafting well-tested software using best practices such as TDD, layered design, dependency injection, and so on. He has contributed to various open source projects and was the creator of JOGRE (Java Online Gaming Real-time Engine).

He is currently the head of engineering at Adoreboard, a unique platform that measures how the world feels about your brand so that marketers can make better business decisions. In his work at Adoreboard, he is a key pioneer for the development of real-time scalable architectures using a combination of technologies, including Enterprise Java, Spring Framework, Cloud computing, and NoSQL databases such as MongoDB, Elasticsearch, Solr, and Redis.

Somanath Nanda has spent the past 3 and a half years in the IT industry developing innovative methods to build new products which can fill the gap between human requirements and technology. He is interested in learning new data usage techniques, high-performance computing, and storage-related technologies. He has worked in various Cloud and big data technologies and data analysis mechanisms. His areas of interest include storage mechanisms of data and new algorithms and computational strategies, followed by high-performance, various machine learning, and data science techniques. Previously, he was involved in reviewing AWS Development Essentials, 1st Ed, 2014.

I would like to thank my parents and friends for their support in making this review successful.

Philip O'Toole has developed software and led software development teams for more than 15 years for a variety of applications including embedded software, networking appliances, web services, and SaaS infrastructure. His most recent work with AWS includes having led the infrastructure design and development of Loggly's log analytics SaaS platform, which is entirely hosted in AWS. He is based in the San Francisco Bay Area and can be found online at `http://www.philipotoole.com`.

Fred Stluka is an avid computer programmer and has been a mentor to hundreds of people over his 30 plus years of professional experience. He is proud to be a "Fred" in the very best sense of the word. For more information, see `http://bristle.com/~fred/MaximizingTheFredFactor.htm`.

He wrote his first book in 1991, `http://archive.adaic.com/docs/style-guide/83style/style-t.txt`.

www.PacktPub.com

Support files, eBooks, discount offers, and more

For support files and downloads related to your book, please visit www.PacktPub.com.

Did you know that Packt offers eBook versions of every book published, with PDF and ePub files available? You can upgrade to the eBook version at www.PacktPub.com and as a print book customer, you are entitled to a discount on the eBook copy. Get in touch with us at service@packtpub.com for more details.

At www.PacktPub.com, you can also read a collection of free technical articles, sign up for a range of free newsletters, and receive exclusive discounts and offers on Packt books and eBooks.

https://www2.packtpub.com/books/subscription/packtlib

Do you need instant solutions to your IT questions? PacktLib is Packt's online digital book library. Here, you can search, access, and read Packt's entire library of books.

Why subscribe?

- Fully searchable across every book published by Packt
- Copy and paste, print, and bookmark content
- On demand and accessible via a web browser

Free access for Packt account holders

If you have an account with Packt at www.PacktPub.com, you can use this to access PacktLib today and view 9 entirely free books. Simply use your login credentials for immediate access.

Table of Contents

Preface

Amazon Web Services (AWS) is arguably the most cutting-edge Cloud provider currently available. In the past, data centers were massive entities that often required days to provide resources for applications. With AWS, this barrier is nonexistent. Applications can be scaled almost instantly. Metrics can be gathered with little or no configuration. Moving into the Cloud, however, might not be easy.

This book will act as a small reference guide, with detailed implementation examples, to show how (and how not) to design your applications in a way that makes them tolerant of underlying hardware failures, resilient against an unexpected influx of data, and easy to manage and replicate. You will be able to see both the benefits and limitations of the current services available to you from the AWS infrastructure.

What this book covers

Chapter 1, Introduction, introduces you to AWS and the problems encountered when deploying and maintaining applications in the Cloud. Problems include upgrading databases, data replication, cache issues, and zero downtime SLAs.

Chapter 2, Basic Patterns, demonstrates some examples of basic patterns such as scaling instances, dynamic disk allocation, and more.

Chapter 3, Patterns for High Availability, demonstrates some examples of patterns for highly available services such as data center replication, floating IP address allocation, health checking, and more.

Chapter 4, Patterns for Processing Static Data, demonstrates some examples of patterns for static data such as cache distribution, direct hosting, web storage hosting, and more.

Chapter 5, Patterns for Processing Dynamic Data, demonstrates some examples of patterns for dynamic data such as state sharing, URL rewriting, rewrite/cache proxying, and more.

Chapter 6, Patterns for Uploading Data, provides some examples of patterns and solutions for object uploading, storage indexing, and write proxying.

Chapter 7, Patterns for Databases, provides some examples of patterns for data replication, in-memory caching, and sharding.

Chapter 8, Patterns for Data Processing, provides some examples of patterns for batch processing issues such as queuing chains, priority queues, and job observers.

Chapter 9, Patterns for Operation and Maintenance, provides some examples of patterns for server swapping, startup settings, backup patterns, and others.

Chapter 10, Patterns for Networking, provides some examples of patterns for multiload balancers, operational and functional firewalls, and on-demand NAT networking.

Chapter 11, Throw-away Environments, is the closing chapter and provides some examples of third-party tools such as CloudFormation, Terraform, and so on, which aid in infrastructure design.

What you need for this book

- An Amazon AWS account
- A modern web browser such as Chrome, Safari, or Firefox
- An SSH client such as Putty

Who this book is for

This book is aimed at architects, solution providers, and those members of the DevOps community who are looking to implement repeatable patterns for deploying and maintaining services in the Amazon Cloud infrastructure. This book could be used by those new to the DevOps movement, as well as those who have embraced the movement and are looking to create reusable patterns. However, prior experience using AWS is required as the book focuses more on the patterns and not on the basics of using AWS.

Conventions

In this book, you will find a number of styles of text that distinguish between different kinds of information. Here are some examples of these styles, and an explanation of their meaning.

Code words in text, database table names, folder names, filenames, file extensions, pathnames, dummy URLs, user input, and Twitter handles are shown as follows:"Once this volume is available, attach it as /dev/sdb to the instance."

A block of code is set as follows:

```
<!doctype html>
<html lang="en">
<head>
    <meta charset="utf-8" />
```

When we wish to draw your attention to a particular part of a code block, the relevant lines or items are set in bold:

```
echo el_s3_getTemporaryLink('MY_ACCESS_KEY', 'MY_SECRET_KEY',
                            'a6408e3f-bc3b-4dab-9749-3cb5aa449bf6',
                            'importantstuff.zip');
```

Any command-line input or output is written as follows:

```
[ec2-user@ip-10-203-10-123 ~]$ TEMP_URL=$(curl --silent -X POST -d
"username=admin&password=legit" http://10.203.10.123/register.php)
[ec2-user@ip-10-203-10-123 ~]$ curl -sL -w "%{http_code}\\n" $TEMP_URL
200
[ec2-user@ip-10-203-10-123 ~]$ sleep 301 && curl -sL -w "%{http_code}\\n"
$TEMP_URL
403
```

New terms and **important words** are shown in bold. Words that you see on the screen, in menus or dialog boxes for example, appear in the text like this: "Clicking the **Next** button moves you to the next screen".

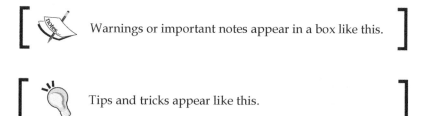

> Warnings or important notes appear in a box like this.

> Tips and tricks appear like this.

Reader feedback

Feedback from our readers is always welcome. Let us know what you think about this book—what you liked or may have disliked. Reader feedback is important for us to develop titles that you really get the most out of.

To send us general feedback, simply send an e-mail to feedback@packtpub.com, and mention the book title via the subject of your message.

If there is a topic that you have expertise in and you are interested in either writing or contributing to a book, see our author guide on www.packtpub.com/authors.

Customer support

Now that you are the proud owner of a Packt book, we have a number of things to help you to get the most from your purchase.

Downloading the example code

You can download the example code files for all Packt books you have purchased from your account at http://www.packtpub.com. If you purchased this book elsewhere, you can visit http://www.packtpub.com/support and register to have the files e-mailed directly to you.

Errata

Although we have taken every care to ensure the accuracy of our content, mistakes do happen. If you find a mistake in one of our books—maybe a mistake in the text or the code—we would be grateful if you would report this to us. By doing so, you can save other readers from frustration and help us improve subsequent versions of this book. If you find any errata, please report them by visiting http://www.packtpub.com/submit-errata, selecting your book, clicking on the **errata submission form** link, and entering the details of your errata. Once your errata are verified, your submission will be accepted and the errata will be uploaded on our website, or added to any list of existing errata, under the Errata section of that title. Any existing errata can be viewed by selecting your title from http://www.packtpub.com/support.

To view the previously submitted errata, go to https://www.packtpub.com/books/content/support and enter the name of the book in the search field. The required information will appear under the **Errata** section.

Piracy

Piracy of copyright material on the Internet is an ongoing problem across all media. At Packt, we take the protection of our copyright and licenses very seriously. If you come across any illegal copies of our works, in any form, on the Internet, please provide us with the location address or website name immediately so that we can pursue a remedy.

Please contact us at copyright@packtpub.com with a link to the suspected pirated material.

We appreciate your help in protecting our authors, and our ability to bring you valuable content.

Questions

You can contact us at questions@packtpub.com if you are having a problem with any aspect of the book, and we will do our best to address it.

1
Introduction

The paradigm for development of applications has shifted in many ways over the years. Instead of just developing pure applications, aimed at specific system configurations, the trend has moved towards web applications. These applications present a very different set of challenges not just for the developers, but also for the people who manage the systems that host them. The reaction to this need to build, test, and manage such web applications has been to develop an abstraction on top of the hardware that allows for the ability to bring up entire virtualized environments quickly and consistently.

Throughout these chapters, you will learn basic design principles for applications and known issues. These may not be completely compatible with all application types but should serve as a basic toolkit for bigger design patterns. It is also very important to note that AWS adds new services all the time, some of which by default solve these design patterns at the time of writing. If your software or services handle sensitive data and have in-flight or at-rest requirements, be very careful to read how each individual AWS-provided service handles data.

The topics that are covered in this chapter are:

- Introduction to AWS
- Cloud computing service models
- Benefits of moving to the Cloud
- Problems encountered with AWS

Introduction to AWS

Amazon Web Services (AWS) is a very large suite of Cloud services provided by Amazon. AWS provides, at a base level, virtual machines and the services surrounding them. Many Cloud-based virtual machine services such as Google Compute Engine, DigitalOcean, Rackspace, Windows Azure, and so on provide the ability to bring up a machine from a supported base operating system image or snapshot, and it's up to the user to customize it further.

Amazon has made itself one of the leaders for Cloud-hosting by providing not just virtual machines, but configurable services and software implementations of hardware found in data centers. For most large-scale systems, the move to Cloud infrastructure brings to the table a huge set of questions on how to handle issues such as load balancing, content delivery networks, failover, and replication. The AWS suite can handle the same issues that a physical data center can, usually for a fraction of the cost. They can get rid of some of the red tape that comes with a data center such as requesting provisioning, repairs, and scheduling downtime.

Amazon is constantly offering new services to tackle new and unique problems encountered with Cloud infrastructure. However, this book may not cover every service offered by Amazon. The services that this book will cover include:

- Computing and networking
    - **Elastic Cloud Compute (EC2)** virtual machines
    - Route 53 DNS provides local and global DNS look-ups
    - **Virtual Private Cloud (VPC)** isolated Cloud networks provide internal networks
    - **Elastic Load Balancers (ELB)** automatically distribute traffic across EC2 instances
    - **Auto Scaling Groups (ASG)** provide a way to scale instances up and down based on schedules or metrics gathered via CloudWatch from the EC2 instances attached to them

- Database
    - SimpleDB is a highly scalable NoSQL database
    - **Relational Database Service (RDS)** is a scalable SQL database apart from MySQL, Oracle, PostgreSQL, or SQL Server
    - ElastiCache is an in-memory cache on top of Redis or MemCached

- Storage and content delivery
    - **Simple Storage Service (S3)** is a distributed storage network that crosses data center boundaries with built-in redundancy
    - CloudFront is a CDN that distributes content based on latency or location

- Application services
    - **Simple Queue Service (SQS)** is a fast, reliable, scalable, and fully managed message queuing service

- Deployment and management
    - CloudFormation is a service that allows the provisioning and updating of AWS resources through templates, usually JSON

- Logging
    - CloudWatch can monitor, display, and alert on instance metrics and logs

 For information on other services provided by AWS that are not relevant to the information in this book visit `http://aws. amazon.com/products/`.

Cloud computing service models

AWS falls under the category of Cloud computing called Infrastructure as a Service. In Cloud computing there are three service models:

- **Infrastructure as a Service (IaaS)**
- **Platform as a Service (PaaS)**
- **Software as a Service (SaaS)**

Infrastructure as a Service

IaaS can be described as a service that provides virtual abstractions for hardware, servers, and networking components. The service provider owns all the equipment and is responsible for its housing, running, and maintenance. In this case, AWS provides APIs, SDKs, and a UI for creating and modifying virtual machines, their network components, routers, gateways, subnets, load balancers, and much more. Where a user with a physical data center would incur charges for the hardware, shelving, and access, this is removed by IaaS with a payment model that is per-hour (or per-use) type.

Platform as a Service

While AWS itself is an IaaS provider, it contains a product named ElasticBeanstalk, which falls under the PaaS category for Cloud models. PaaS is described as the delivery of a computing platform, typically an operating system, programming language execution environment, database, or web server. With ElasticBeanStalk, a user can easily turn a code into a running environment without having to worry about any of the pieces underneath such as setting up and maintaining the database, web server, or code runtime versions. It also allows it to be scaled without having to do anything other than define scale policies through the configuration.

Software as a Service

AWS also provides a marketplace where a user can purchase official and third-party operating system images that provide configurable services such as databases, web applications, and more. This type of service falls under the SaaS model. The best interpretation for the SaaS model is on-demand software, meaning that the user need only configure the software to use and interact with it. The draw to SaaS is that there is no need to learn how to configure and deploy the software to get it working in a larger stack and generally the charges are per usage-hour.

The AWS suite is both impressive and unique in that it doesn't fall under any one of the Cloud service models as described previously. Until AWS made its name, the need to virtualize an entire environment or stack was usually not an easy task and consisted of a collection of different providers, each solving a specific part of the deployment puzzle. The cost of using many different providers to create a virtual stack might not be cheaper than the initial hardware cost for moving equipment into a data center. Besides the cost of the providers themselves, having multiple providers also created the problem of scaling in one area and notifying another of the changes. While making applications more resilient and scalable, this Frankenstein method usually did not simplify the problem as a whole.

Benefits of moving to the Cloud

There are many different answers to why moving to a Cloud-hosted environment might be beneficial but it depends on the end user. The shift may suit small teams but for mid-sized teams the effort saved begins to outweigh the cost. I start at mid-sized because this is the size that usually includes the two teams that benefit the most:

- The developers and testers
- Operations

For a developer, the biggest benefit of Cloud providers is the ability to throw away entire environments. In a traditional developer setting, the developers usually develop their code locally, have access to a shared physical server, or have access to a virtual server of some type. Issues that usually arise out of these setups are that it's hard to enforce consistency and the servers can become stale over time. If each developer works locally, inconsistency can arise very quickly. Different versions of the core language or software could be used and might behave differently from machine to machine. One developer might use Windows and prefer registry look-ups while another developer may use Mac and prefer environment variables.

If the developers share a core server for development, other issues may arise such as permissions or possibly trying to modify services independent of each other causing race conditions. No matter what problems exist, known or unknown, they could be solved by always starting from the same base operating system state. The leading software for solving this issue is Vagrant. Vagrant provides the ability to spin up and destroy a virtual machine from a configuration file along with a configuration management suite such as Puppet, Chef, Docker, or Ansible. Vagrant itself is agnostic to the Cloud hosting tool in the sense that it does not require AWS. It can spin up instances at AWS given the credentials, but it can also spin up virtual machines locally from VirtualBox and VMWare.

Vagrant gives back consistency to the developers in the sense that it takes a base box (in AWS terms this is an Amazon Machine Image or AMI) and configures it via one of the configuration suites or shell to create a running virtual machine every time it is needed. If all the developers share the same configuration file then all of them are mostly guaranteed to work against the same environment. That environment can be destroyed just as easily as it was created, giving the resources back and incurring no charges until needed again.

The bringing up and destroying of the instances becomes a small invisible piece of their workflow. By virtue of enforcing a strategy like this on a team, a lot of issues can be found and resolved before they make their way up the chain to the testing or production environments.

[More information on Vagrant can be found at http://www.vagrantup.com.]

The other team I mentioned that benefits from moving to the Cloud is the operations team. This team differs greatly in responsibility from company to company but it is safe to assume that the team is heavily involved with monitoring the applications and systems for issues and possible optimizations. AWS provides enough infrastructure for monitoring and acting on metrics and an entire book could be dedicated to the topic. However, I'll focus only on auto scaling groups and CloudWatch.

For AWS, an auto scaling group defines scaling policies for instances based on schedules, custom metrics, or base metrics such as disk usage, CPU utilization, memory usage, and so on. An auto scaling group can act on these thresholds and scale up or down depending on how they are configured. In a non-Cloud environment this same setup takes quite a bit of effort and depends on the software whereas, it's a core concept to AWS.

Auto scaling groups also automatically register instances with a load balancer and shift them into a round robin distribution. For an operations team, the benefit of moving to Amazon might justify itself only to alleviate all the work involved in duplicating this functionality elsewhere, allowing the team to focus on creating deeper and more meaningful system health checks.

Throw-away environments can also be beneficial to the operations teams. A sibling product to Vagrant, very recently released, is Terraform. Terraform, like Vagrant, is agnostic to the hosting environment but does not solely spin up virtual instances. Terraform is similar to CloudFormation in the sense that its goal is to take a central configuration file, which describes all the resources it needs. It then maps them into a dependency graph, optimizes, and creates an entire stack. A common example for Terraform would be to create a production environment from a few virtual machines, load balancers, Route53 DNS entries, and set auto scaling policies. This flexibility would be nearly impossible in traditional hardware settings and provides an on-demand mentality not just for the base application, but also for the entire infrastructure, leading to a more agile core.

[ More information on Terraform can be found at
`http://www.terraform.io`.]

Common problems encountered at AWS

The previous sections have tried to make light of issues found in traditional settings, which might make moving to a Cloud infrastructure seem like a logical choice with no ramifications. But this is not true. While Cloud infrastructure aims to resolve many problems, it does bring up new issues to the user.

Underlying hardware failures

Some issues can be avoided while others may not. Some examples of issues that may not be avoided, other than user error, are underlying hardware issues that propagate themselves to the user. Hardware has a fail rate and can be guaranteed to fail at some point while the benefit of IaaS is that, even though the hardware is abstracted away, it is still a relevant topic to anyone using it.

AWS has a **Service Level Agreement (SLA)** policy for each service, which guarantees that at their end you will meet a certain percentage of uptime. This implies a certain amount of downtime for scheduled maintenance and repairs of the hardware underneath.

As an AWS user this means you can expect an e-mail at some point during usage warning about instances being stopped and the need to restart manually. While this is no different from a physical environment where the user schedules their own downtime, it does mean that instances can misbehave when the hardware is starting to fail. Most of the replication and failover is handled underneath but if the application is real-time and is stopped, it does mean that you, as a user, should have policies in place to handle this situation.

Over-provisioning

Another issue with having virtual machines in the Cloud is over-provisioning. An instance type is selected when an instance is launched that corresponds to the virtualized hardware required for it. Without taking measures to ensure that replication or scaling happens on multiple data centers, there is a very real risk that when a new instance is needed, the hardware will not be immediately available. If scaling policies are in effect that specify your application should scale out to a certain number of instances, but all of those instances are in a data center nearing its maximum capacity, the scaling policy will fail. This failure negates having a scaling policy in place if it cannot always scale to the size required.

Under-provisioning

A topic that is rarely talked about but is very common is under-provisioning and it is the opposite of over-provisioning. We will start with an example: say we purchase a server for hosting a database and purchase the smallest instance type possible. Let's assume that for the next few days this is the only machine running in a specific rack in the AWS data center. We are promised the resources of the instance we purchased but as the hardware is free, it gives us a boost in performance that we get accustomed to unknowingly.

After a few days, the hardware that has been provisioned for other customers, now gives us the resources we were promised and not the extra boost we got for free in the background. While monitoring we now see a performance degradation! While this database was originally able to perform so many transactions per second it now does much less. The problem here is that we grew accustomed to the processing power that technically was not ours and now our database does not perform the way we expected it to.

Perhaps the promised amount is not suitable but it is live and has customer data within it. To resolve this, we must terminate the instance and change the instance type to something more powerful, which could have downstream effects or even full downtime to the customer. This is the danger of under-provisioning and it is extremely hard to trace. Not knowing what kind of a performance we should actually get (as promised in the SLA) causes us to possibly affect the customer, which is never ideal.

Replication

The previous examples are extreme and rarely encountered. For example, in a traditional hosting environment where there are multiple applications behind a load balancer, replication is not trivial. Replication of this application server requires registration with the load balancer and is usually done manually or requires configuration each time. AWS-provided ELBs are a first-class entity just like the virtual machines themselves. The registration between this is abstracted and can be done with the click of a button or automatically through auto scaling groups and start-up scripts.

Redundancy

Apart from replication, redundancy is another hot topic. Most database clustering takes redundancy into effect but requires special configuration and initial setup. The RDS allows replication to be specified at the time of setup and guarantees redundancy and uptime as per its SLA. Their Multi-AZ specification guarantees that the replication crosses availability zones and provides automatic failover. Besides replication, special software or configuration is needed to store offsite backups. With S3, an instance may synchronize with an S3 bucket. S3 is itself a redundant storage that crosses data center sites and can be done via an AWS CLI or their provided API. S3 is also a first-class entity so permissions can be provided transparently to virtual machines.

The previous database example hints towards a set of issues deemed high availability. The purpose of high availability is to mitigate redundancy through a load balancer, proxy, or crossing availability zones. This is a part of risk management and disaster recovery. The last thing an operations team would want is to have their database go down and be replicated to New Orleans during Hurricane Katrina. This is an extreme and incredibly rare example but the risk exists. The reason that disaster recovery exists and will always exist is the simple fact that accidents happen and have happened when ill-prepared.

Improving the end user experience

Another set of problems to be solved is optimization to the end user. Optimization in this case is proxying through cache servers so that high workloads can be handled without spinning up more instances. In a scaling policy, high bandwidth would lead to more instances, which incur cost and startup time. Caching static content, where possible, can help mitigate high bandwidth peaks. Other ways to optimize without caching might be to use Content Delivery Networks (CDNs) such as the AWS-provided CloudFront service, which automatically choose servers geographically close to the user.

Monitoring and log-gathering

The last set of problems to discuss in small detail is operational in nature. Most applications generate logs and large software stacks with many disparate logs. Third-party software such as Loggly and Splunk exist to aggregate and search log collections but AWS has services dedicated to this as well. The preferred way is to upload logs to CloudWatch. CloudWatch allows you to directly search and create alerts on the data within logs. Since CloudWatch is a first-class AWS service, they provide an SLA similar to the instance itself and the storage is scalable.

These are only some of the issues that someone shifting into AWS might encounter or need to fortify their infrastructure against. Reading through the chapters of this book will serve as a beginner's guide of sorts to help create a resilient infrastructure against these issues and others.

Summary

Throughout this brief introduction to AWS, we learned not only the background and industry shift into virtualized infrastructure, but also where AWS fits in with some competitors. We not only discussed the kinds of problems AWS solves, but also the kinds of problems that can be encountered in Cloud infrastructure. There are countless unique processes to be solved with this dynamic paravirtual environment. Picking up consistent patterns throughout this book will help to strengthen applications of many forms against these issues. In the next chapter, we will go over some basic design patterns. It is one of the easier topics and covers data backups through instance snapshots, replication through machine imaging, scaling instance types, dynamic scaling through CloudWatch, and increasing the disk size when needed. These patterns help solve common provisioning issues for single instances.

2
Basic Patterns

The first patterns we will learn are considered to be the most rudimentary patterns for Cloud infrastructure. Many patterns throughout this book will be very heavily tied to AWS-specific services while the patterns here can be applied in many other Cloud virtualization infrastructures that have similar capabilities. In this chapter we will cover the following topics:

- Snapshot pattern
- Stamp pattern
- Scale up pattern
- Scale out pattern
- On-demand disk pattern

For this chapter, I will use the Amazon provided and supported **Amazon Machine Image (AMI)** titled **Amazon Linux AMI**. The base AMI that you choose or the machine type to launch the AMI is not important for this chapter, as long as it is a Linux image. Images based on Windows have some inconsistencies and require special steps to be taken to create reusable images and snapshots. While following along, if you decide to use an alternate image, the code snippets may not work as expected.

 For more information on the Amazon-curated Linux AMI, visit
`http://aws.amazon.com/amazon-linux-ami/`.

With AWS there is some redundancy built into image volumes. Volumes can be thought of as hardware disk drives as far as the operating system is concerned, and can be added and removed freely. The volumes have built-in redundancy over the hardware underneath them, but are not replicated across availability zones. If the hardware fails, the drives will keep their data but if the data center goes down, the data will be lost.

To prevent loss of data, we should look at ways to secure the volumes themselves. In a traditional data center, there is no single way to back up data. The data could be backed up from software such as Acronis or Norton Ghost and stored on a separate server. From a Cloud perspective, there is always a service provided to do this and AWS calls it hard drive snapshots.

A snapshot is the state of a system at a point in time similar to the **Logical Unit Number (LUN)** level copies of data. When a snapshot is created, the data is stored in S3, away from the users' perspective.

A snapshot can be created at will but that does not mean that the data is usable from a user or system perspective. An example of this would be creating a snapshot of a volume that is currently doing high read/write operations such as a database. Creating a snapshot should be done at points where I/O is at a minimum state and no file locks exist, to ensure that any volumes created from these snapshots do not have inconsistencies or issues during a recovery operation.

The reader might note that if the volume being snapshotted is a root volume from which the system was booted, it can be turned into a bootable AMI. If the volume is not bootable, such as a data volume, it cannot be turned into an AMI. The AWS console helps this process by only allowing the user to create an AMI from an instance as the assumption is that the instance has a bootable disk.

Introducing Vagrant

Throughout this book, the user will be creating running instances to follow along. The AWS console is suitable for all examples, as well as Vagrant, and will be demonstrated as such.

Vagrant, as described in the introduction, is a piece of software that has a configuration file, or Vagrantfile, which describes how to run a virtual machine under a provider. Vagrant, by default, does not have the AWS provider built in and requires a plugin Vagrant-AWS. To install Vagrant, download the latest version from their website http://www.vagrantup.com and install it as described in their HOWTO.

Once Vagrant is installed correctly, the AWS plugin can be installed as follows:

```
$ vagrant plugin install vagrant-aws
Installing the 'vagrant-aws' plugin. This can take a few minutes...
Installed the plugin 'vagrant-aws (0.5.0)'!
```

Every provider for Vagrant requires a base box, which is not applicable for AWS. A box file is a compressed virtual machine disk with its configuration. For example, with Virtualbox or Parallels it would be the configuration files and the **virtual machine disk file (VMDK)**. Because we cannot get access to a Linux AMI, as it is hosted entirely in the AWS infrastructure, the author of the plugin states to create a dummy box so that Vagrant can proceed as the API call uses an AMI described in the configuration file. To add this dummy box, the following can be run:

```
$ vagrant box add dummy https://github.com/mitchellh/vagrant-aws/raw/
master/dummy.box

==> box: Adding box 'dummy' (v0) for provider:
    box: Downloading: https://github.com/mitchellh/vagrant-aws/raw/
master/dummy.box
    box:
==> box: Successfully added box 'dummy' (v0) for 'aws'!
```

If you wish to follow along using Vagrant, create a file called Vagrantfile with contents similar to the following.

 Please note that you, the reader, would provide the necessary configuration such as access key, secret key, SSH private key location, and so on:

```
Vagrant.configure("2") do |config|
  config.vm.box = "dummy"

  config.vm.provider :aws do |aws, override|
    aws.access_key_id = "MYACCESSKEY"
    aws.instance_type = "t2.micro"
    aws.secret_access_key = "MYSECRETKEY"
    aws.keypair_name = "MYKEYPAIR"

    #The AMI ID for 'Amazon Linux AMI 2014.09.1 (HVM)'
    aws.ami = "ami-b66ed3de"
    override.ssh.username = "ec2-user"
    override.ssh.private_key_path = "~/.ssh/mykey"
  end
end
```

After these steps are performed, an instance can be launched in EC2 by issuing the command:

```
$ vagrant up --provider aws
```

By default, the Amazon provided Linux AMI does not directly work with Vagrant. Vagrant requires `sudo` to work properly and does not work without a TTY unless explicitly enabled in their AMI. We demonstrate how to resolve this in the *Stamp pattern* section but it is described in more detail on the Vagrant wiki at `https://github.com/mitchellh/vagrant-aws/wiki/Amazon-Linux-AMI`.

Snapshot pattern

The first basic pattern that we will cover is the snapshot pattern. This pattern is the basis for many other patterns described throughout this book and includes the way to create an S3-backed, point-in-time snapshot of a running instance from the AWS console. To do this, we will select a running instance from the EC2 console and select the root device volume from the instance pull-up frame, which will bring up a pop-up for the volume as shown in the following screenshot:

Click the **EBS ID** link from the pop-up. This will bring you to the **Volumes** section of the AWS console with the previously selected volume in context. From here, select the **Actions** drop-down and select **Create Snapshot** as shown in the following screenshot:

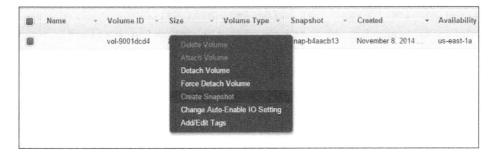

You will now be prompted for a name and description, but they are optional so go ahead and click **Create**. The next window will give you a success prompt with a snapshot identifier. If you select the snapshot id, it will take you to the **Snapshot** section of the AWS console where you may monitor the operation. Depending on how long AWS takes to process the request, as well as the size of the volume, this operation could take several seconds or several minutes.

From here, you have a restore point of sorts. The volume to the instance can tolerate some level of failure underneath, while the snapshot created can tolerate much more including failover. Since we created a snapshot from a root volume, we could create an AMI from it and create an instance identical to the original. That leads us into the stamp pattern.

Stamp pattern

The pattern covered here is called the stamp pattern because it covers how to replicate a bootable operating system similar to a rubber stamp of sorts. By creating an image of an operating system that is pre-configured for a purpose, it can be easily replicated by simply bringing it up when needed in the same way a stamp works by creating a template.

We will actually create a new AMI to use throughout this book from this method. The AWS Linux AMI, by default, does not allow sudo without a TTY terminal. There's a simple fix for this but it must be run every time we boot from the AWS Linux AMI unmodified. Instead, we will make this fix to their image and package it into our own AMI.

This is useful because Vagrant requires sudo to be usable for many of its features such as folder synchronization, and provisioners such as Puppet and Chef. If you were to try to run Vagrant on their base AMI, you would get an output such as:

```
$ vagrant up --provider aws
Bringing machine 'default' up with 'aws' provider...
==> default: Launching an instance with the following settings...
==> default:    -- Type: t2.micro
==> default:    -- AMI: ami-b66ed3de
==> default:    -- Region: us-east-1
==> default:    -- Keypair: cdr-pcs
==> default:    -- Subnet ID: subnet-25383163
==> default:    -- Security Groups: ["sg-621b8807", "sg-e814878d"]
==> default:    -- Block Device Mapping: []
==> default:    -- Terminate On Shutdown: false
==> default:    -- Monitoring: false
==> default:    -- EBS optimized: false
==> default:    -- Assigning a public IP address in a VPC: false
==> default: Waiting for instance to become "ready"...
==> default: Waiting for SSH to become available...
==> default: Machine is booted and ready for use!
==> default: Rsyncing folder: /cygdrive/C/Users/myoung/repos/book => /
vagrant
```

The following ssh command responded with a non-zero exit status.

Vagrant assumes that this means the command failed!

```
mkdir -p '/vagrant'
Stdout from the command:
Stderr from the command:
sudo: sorry, you must have a tty to run sudo
```

To resolve this, launch a running instance from the AWS Linux AMI in the AWS console. Once it is running ssh into it, proceed to run:

```
[ec2-user@ip-10-203-10-45 ~]$ sudo su -
[root@ip-10-203-10-45 ~]# echo 'Defaults:ec2-user !requiretty' > /etc/
sudoers.d/999-vagrant-cloud-init-requiretty
[root@ip-10-203-10-45 ~]# chmod 440 /etc/sudoers.d/999-vagrant-cloud-
init-requiretty
```

Once this is complete, we can prove that Vagrant will behave by running the 'provision' command. This will re-run all provisioners, including the `rsync`, which failed earlier. Now that the fix has been made, Vagrant should behave as:

```
$ vagrant provision
default: Rsyncing folder: /Users/myoung/repos/book/ => /vagrant
```

Once we have made a change to the running instance, we will create an AMI from it. To do that, first locate the running instance in the AWS console, and select **Create Image** from the **Actions** drop-down.

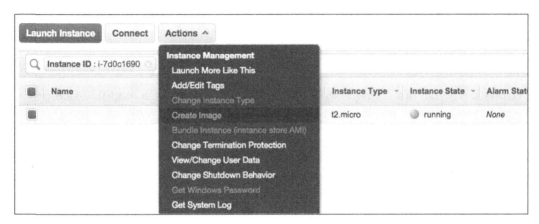

After you select **Create Image,** it will ask you for a name and description. Name is required, but description is optional so name it `AWS Linux AMI - vagrant`, and click **Create Image**. You will be greeted with a confirmation prompt that has the AMI ID for the new image. If you click on this identifier, it will take you to the AMI property of the AWS console, with the context set to the image you created. Once the status changes to available, we are ready to proceed. Also note that, just like snapshots, the time it takes to create the image could take anywhere from a few seconds to several minutes. From the command line where we used Vagrant to create the running, we will terminate the instance:

```
$ vagrant destroy -f
default: Terminating the instance...
```

Now that the instance is terminated and we have a new AMI to work from as a stamp, we will modify the `Vagrantfile` that we created to use the AMI ID of the `AWS Linux AMI - vagrant` that we created. It should resemble the following code:

```
Vagrant.configure("2") do |config|
  config.vm.box = "dummy"
```

```
config.vm.provider :aws do |aws, override|
  aws.access_key_id = "MYACCESSKEY"
  aws.instance_type = "t2.micro"
  aws.secret_access_key = "MYSECRETKEY"
  aws.keypair_name = "MYKEYPAIR"

  #The AMI ID for 'Amazon Linux AMI - vagrant'
  aws.ami = "ami-f8840f90"
  override.ssh.username = "ec2-user"
  override.ssh.private_key_path = "~/.ssh/mykey"
  end
end
```

To check whether our changes worked, and that we now have a modified stamp AMI to work from, we will create a new running instance. Run the vagrant command again. It should succeed with no errors, as shown:

```
$ vagrant up --provider aws
Bringing machine 'default' up with 'aws' provider...
==> default: Launching an instance with the following settings...
==> default:   -- Type: t2.micro
==> default:   -- AMI: ami-f8840f90
==> default:   -- Region: us-east-1
==> default:   -- Keypair: cdr-pcs
==> default:   -- Subnet ID: subnet-25383163
==> default:   -- Security Groups: ["sg-621b8807", "sg-e814878d"]
==> default:   -- Block Device Mapping: []
==> default:   -- Terminate On Shutdown: false
==> default:   -- Monitoring: false
==> default:   -- EBS optimized: false
==> default:   -- Assigning a public IP address in a VPC: false
==> default: Waiting for instance to become "ready"...
==> default: Waiting for SSH to become available...
==> default: Machine is booted and ready for use!
==> default: Rsyncing folder: /Users/myoung/repos/book/ => /vagrant
```

What we have effectively done is central to any AWS workflow, that is, we made a change to the base image, and packaged it as our own. Many teams that utilize AWS for their systems, manage many AMIs for specific purposes. The concept of creating an AMI to use across this purpose is the stamp pattern.

Scale up pattern

The scale up pattern is a method that allows a server to change size and specifications dynamically, and as needed. Imagine a running web instance that does a bit of computation per request. Initially, it performs extremely well, but over time traffic becomes heavier and causes the computation time to increase. A couple of options exist to solve this problem, but all have their own benefits and issues.

One option could be to spin up a second instance (or scale outwards), but this means double the cost, as well as any maintenance required to be performed on each server. For applications in the Cloud, it is important not only to think of the cost involved in the server, but also the implied costs, such as operational. The easiest solution might be to change the specs on the current server or scaling up. A benefit of this method is that, if the processing peak can be predicted, such as the beginning of the month or the end of the month transactions, this method can be automated by using the AWS-provided API.

There are some cautions to note from this method, however. If the instance is performing poorly in ways that are not due to CPU or RAM usage, for example, this method will not help. Another reason might be that the server cannot afford downtime. For these examples, scaling out instead of up is a better solution.

First we will start up another running instance from either the AWS Linux AMI, or
the Vagrant-compatible AMI. Once it is running, select the instance from the AWS
console, and select **Stop** instance from the **Actions** drop-down, as shown in the
following screenshot:

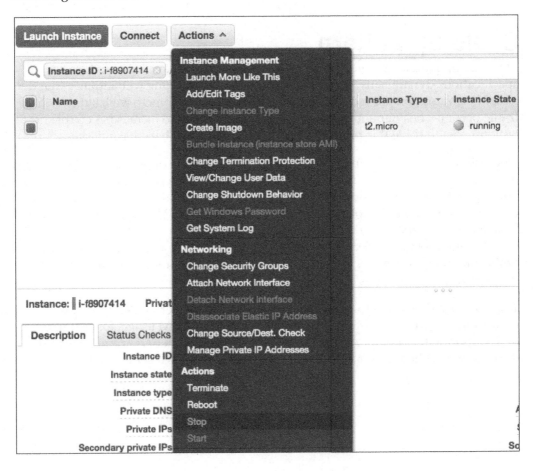

It will prompt you to confirm, so go ahead, and click **Yes Stop**. This will safely shut down the virtual machine. Once this image is stopped, we can now modify the instance type. The previous instance was started as a **t2.micro**, which has 1 GB of RAM. Once stopped, the instance type can now be changed. From the **Actions** drop-down menu, again select **Change Instance Type**.

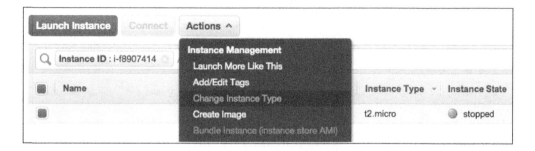

You will now be greeted with a prompt for the type. Select **t2.small** as the type, and click **Apply**.

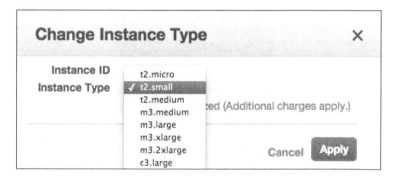

In the AWS console, you will notice that the **Instance Type** column for this instance now shows **t2.small**. Select **Start** instance from the **Actions** drop-down, select **Yes Start** from the confirmation and the instance will begin to start up with the same behavior as before, albeit with 2 GB RAM and a few other differences in the hardware specs.

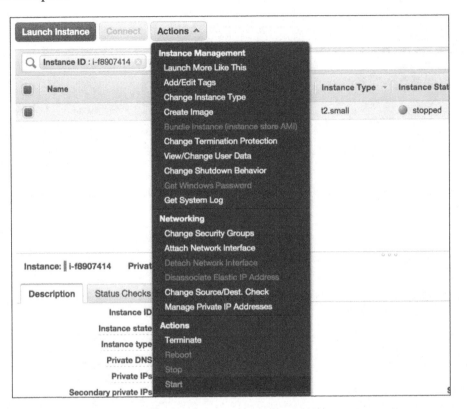

With minimal downtime, we have now made the instance more powerful without incurring any additional cost, aside from the operational cost to ourselves and the difference in the costs between the instance types. At any point in the future this instance can be downgraded in specifications with the same steps to lower the specifications and save on the cost.

Scale out pattern

We have discussed up to this point how to scale up in resources on an instance but not how to scale out. Scaling up an instance can only help in a few limited examples, but the more important issue is how to add processing power without affecting the client or the systems interacting with our services. To do this, we will tie together a few different EC2 resources. The resource diagram, as shown, will help to visualize what we are trying to accomplish:

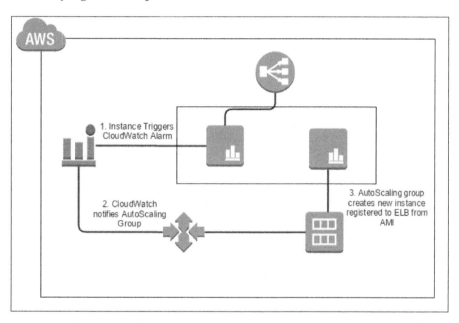

The general process for this pattern is:

- Create an elastic load balancer with forwarding ports and health checks
- Create a launch configuration for the instance
- Create an auto scaling group with configured CloudWatch alarms and scaling policies

To demonstrate this, we will first create an elastic load balancer. Browse to the **Load Balancers** portion of the AWS console and select **Create Load Balancer** as seen in the following screenshot:

At the **Define Load Balancer** prompt, give it a descriptive name in the **Load Balancer Name** text box and set it to listen on port 80 for both the **Load Balancer Port** and the **Instance Port**. Then select **Continue**.

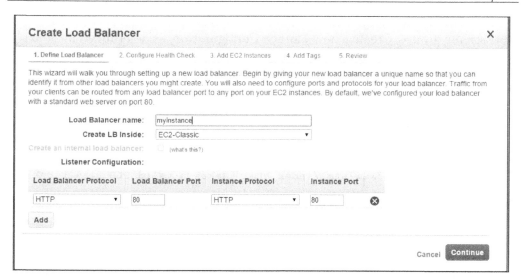

At the **Configure Health Check,** set the **Ping Port** to 80 and set the **Ping Path** to /index.html. Select **Continue,** followed by the rest of the **Add EC2 Instances**, **Add Tags**, and **Review** tabs, to finish creating this load balancer.

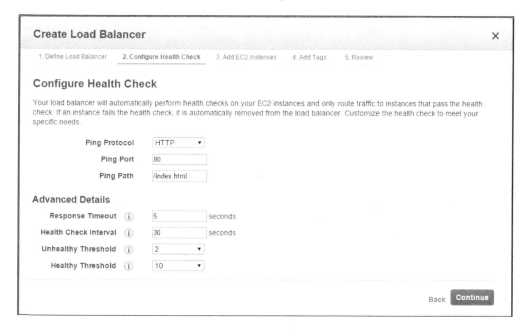

Next, we will browse to the **Launch Configuration** of the AWS console under auto scaling groups. Create a new **Launch Configuration,** as determined by your networking setup including **Instance Type,** but make sure to expand **Advanced Details** on the **Configure details** tab of the creation page. Enable CloudWatch Monitoring and add the user data:

```
#!/bin/bash
yum install -y httpd stress
service iptables stop
echo welcome > /var/www/html/index.html #Makes a valid ELB health chk
service httpd start
```

Next, create a scaling group in the **Create Auto Scaling Group** section of the AWS console, which references the **Launch Configuration** that you just created. Ensure that you enable CloudWatch via the checkbox **Enable CloudWatch detailed monitoring** and set it to receive traffic from the load balancer that you created.

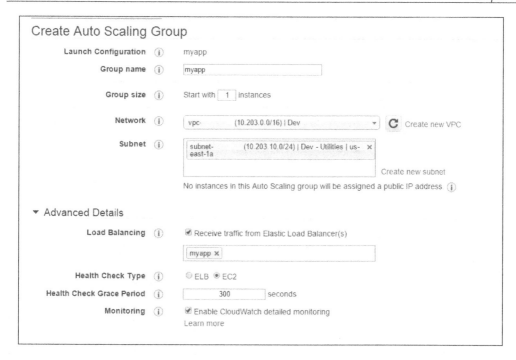

Lastly, before you finish the auto scaling group creation, check the **Use scaling policies to adjust the capacity of this group** radio button in the **Configure scaling policies** tab.

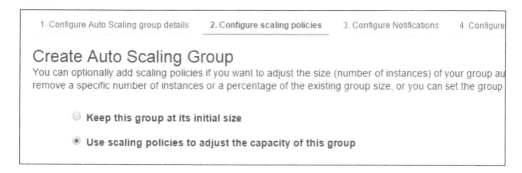

Set the **scale between** option to 1 and 2 instances, respectively. Select the **Add new alarm** button next to the **Increase policy**.

In the **Create Alarm** pop-up tab, create an Increase policy that adds 1 instance if the CPUUtilization metric average is above 75 percent for 1 period(s) of 5 minutes.

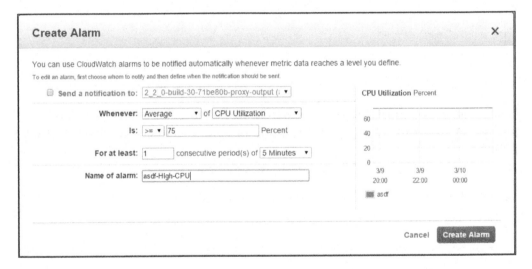

Finally, add a Decrease policy that removes 1 instance if the CPUUtilization metric is below or equal to 25 percent for 3 periods of 1 minute as shown in the following screenshot:

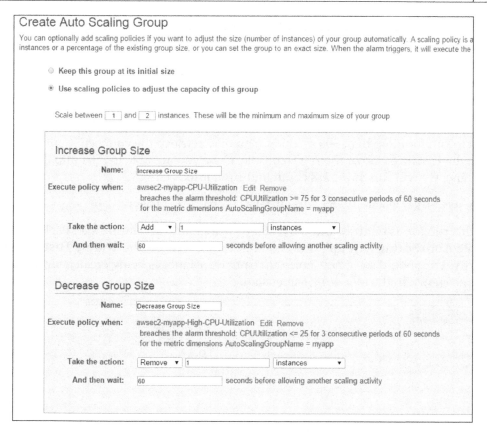

You can proceed as needed to finish the auto scaling group. You will notice after creation that a new instance is beginning to start in the auto scaling groups portion of the AWS console. When it has completed its user data, it will register to the load balancer that you created. Once its status is `InService` in the load balancer, you can confirm that everything is currently configured correctly by browsing to the load balancer's DNS record (located on the main tab for the load balancer in the AWS console).

Here's an example of what you should see using the `curl` command:

```
$ curl --silent http://internal-myapp-652412119.us-east-1.elb.amazonaws.com/
Welcome
```

Now for the fun part: we will test the scaling policy by forcing the CPU of the instance to run at full utilization. We will use the `stress` command to do this and set it to run for more than 300 seconds. You may retrieve the connection information from the **Instances** tab of the AWS console. Once you are able to SSH into this virtual machine, we will run the stress command similar to:

```
[ec2-user@ip-10-203-10-55 ~]$ stress --cpu 1 --timeout 240
```

Let this run for its entirety and the instance will go into an alarm state. Back in the **Create Auto Scaling Group** portion of the console, refresh the **Scaling History** tab. Shortly, you should see a new entry that a new instance is being created similar to the one shown in the following screenshot:

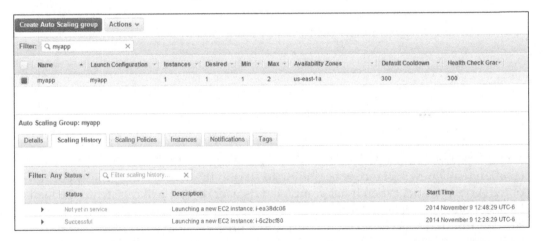

Our stress test caused the CPU utilization to cross our alarm boundary and the auto scaling group increased the size to respond. Here, the new instance will run the same user data as the first instance and register to the load balancer. When the load balancer finishes the health checks, the new instance will be used appropriately to lower the load off the original. By now the `stress` command that we issued has finished, or will finish shortly. Once this has completed and another 180 seconds have passed, the Decrease policy will respond to the CPU utilization being less than 25 percent and terminate the original instance as seen in the following screenshot:

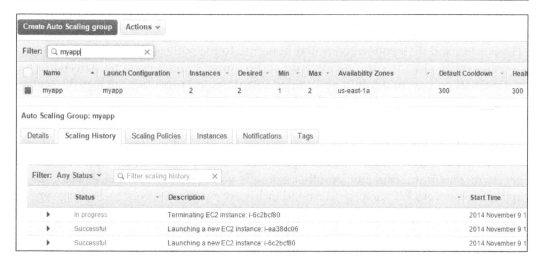

Name		Launch Configuration	Instances	Desired	Min	Max	Availability Zones		Default Cooldown		Healt
myapp		myapp	2	2	1	2	us-east-1a		300		300

Auto Scaling Group: myapp

Details | **Scaling History** | Scaling Policies | Instances | Notifications | Tags

Filter: Any Status ∨ | Q Filter scaling history ✕

	Status	Description	Start Time
▶	In progress	Terminating EC2 instance: i-6c2bcf80	2014 November 9 1
▶	Successful	Launching a new EC2 instance: i-ea38dc06	2014 November 9 1
▶	Successful	Launching a new EC2 instance: i-6c2bcf80	2014 November 9 1

It is important to note at this point that auto scaling groups terminate the oldest instance first, or the instance that is the cheapest to terminate.

The auto scaling termination policy is not quite this simple in practice and is subject to change. The latest information on the termination policy can be found on the documentation page at `http://docs.aws.amazon.com/AutoScaling/latest/DeveloperGuide/AutoScalingBehavior.InstanceTermination.html`.

The newest instance will stay in service for the load balancer to use. This is not an issue for our example, but if your servers require manual processes of any kind, havoc might ensue. We have now successfully configured our system to scale outwards as needed.

This example uses metrics based on CPU utilization that might not be applicable for an HTTP server, such as the one we have configured. CloudWatch enables you to generate metrics based on any parameter you wish, so it might be more relevant, if not more difficult, to generate metrics based on response time, or the number of requests in a given point and alerts on these. Information on publishing custom metrics can be found at the AWS Developer guide at `http://docs.aws.amazon.com/AmazonCloudWatch/latest/DeveloperGuide/publishingMetrics.html`.

On-demand disk pattern

The on-demand disk pattern is similar in nature to the scale up pattern, in that it operates on an already running instance and requires some downtime. This pattern is a manual process and might be avoided in automated processes such as the scale out pattern, as the downtime involved might cause alarm or scaling policies to trigger, causing some unwanted side effects.

The benefit of on-demand disk size is that you do not need to plan ahead for disk resources. Once the instance is running, you can simply resize its volume when it gets to its maximum capacity. Another example would be in the event where your application is very I/O heavy. At first your instance performs very well, but over time, with increased usage, the I/O operations take longer. An easy way to get more performance out of the base volume might be to enable RAID and stripe the volume.

First we will launch the AWS Linux AMI with an additional 20 GB EBS volume. Ensure that the **Volume Type** is `Magnetic` and it is set to **Delete on Termination** as shown in the following screenshot:

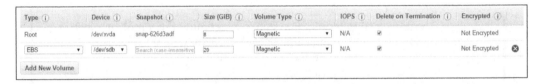

Once it is running, we will need to format and mount the drive for usage. We will mount it to /opt/data:

```
[ec2-user@ip-10-203-10-237 ~]$ sudo su -
Last login: Sun Nov  9 13:32:35 UTC 2014 on pts/0


[root@ip-10-203-10-99 ~]# lsblk # view block devices attached
NAME      MAJ:MIN RM SIZE RO TYPE MOUNTPOINT
xvda      202:0    0   8G  0 disk
└─xvda1   202:1    0   8G  0 part /
xvdb      202:16   0  20G  0 disk


[root@ip-10-203-10-237 ~]# mkfs -t ext4 /dev/xvdb #format the secondary
drive as ext4 filesystem
mke2fs 1.42.9 (28-Dec-2013)
Filesystem label=
OS type: Linux
```

```
Block size=4096 (log=2)

Fragment size=4096 (log=2)

Stride=0 blocks, Stripe width=0 blocks

1310720 inodes, 5242880 blocks

262144 blocks (5.00%) reserved for the super user

First data block=0

Maximum filesystem blocks=2153775104

160 block groups

32768 blocks per group, 32768 fragments per group

8192 inodes per group

Superblock backups stored on blocks:
        32768, 98304, 163840, 229376, 294912, 819200, 884736, 1605632,
2654208,
        4096000


Allocating group tables: done

Writing inode tables: done

Creating journal (32768 blocks): done

Writing superblocks and filesystem accounting information: done


[root@ip-10-203-10-237 ~]# echo $'/dev/xvdb\t/opt/data\text4\
tdefaults,nofail\t0\t2' >> /etc/fstab

[root@ip-10-203-10-237 ~]# mkdir /opt/data && mount /opt/data
```

Now that we have the EBS volume mounted to /opt/data, we will write a file to the disk to ensure that a resize retains the data:

```
[root@ip-10-203-10-99 ~]# time dd if=/dev/zero of=/opt/data/test bs=512k
count=200

200+0 records in

200+0 records out

104857600 bytes (105 MB) copied, 0.0667198 s, 1.6 GB/s


real    0m0.068s

user    0m0.000s

sys     0m0.064s

[root@ip-10-203-10-99 ~]# time dd if=/dev/zero of=/opt/data/test bs=512k
count=200
```

```
200+0 records in
200+0 records out
104857600 bytes (105 MB) copied, 2.63703 s, 39.8 MB/s


real    0m2.648s
user    0m0.000s
sys     0m0.076s
```

Volume resize

First we will unmount the volume from the running instance with the umount command:

```
[root@ip-10-203-10-99 ~]# umount /opt/data
```

After the volume is unmounted, select the instance from the console, and select the **20 GiB** drive attached as /dev/sdb. This will take you to the corresponding volume in the **Volumes** section of the console. Click the **Actions** drop-down, and select **Create Snapshot,** as described in the snapshot pattern. Once this snapshot is 100 percent available for use, detach the /dev/sdb volume from the instance as shown in the following screenshot:

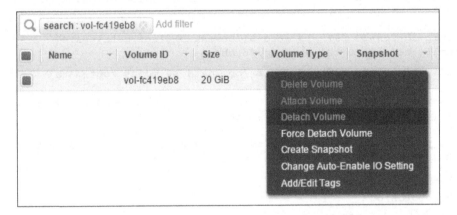

To increase the size of the volume, select the snapshot, and select **Create Volume** from the **Actions** menu. Here, select a larger size such as 30 GB, and click **Create**. When the new volume is available, click **Attach Volume** from the **Actions** menu, and select the instance that we detached, ensuring you attach it back to the device we detached it from, or in this case /dev/sdb. Back inside the virtual machine, you will remount the device, check it for errors, resize the partition, check the new size, and ensure that we didn't lose any data:

```
[root@ip-10-203-10-99 ~]# lsblk # view block devices attached
NAME      MAJ:MIN RM SIZE RO TYPE MOUNTPOINT
xvda      202:0    0   8G  0 disk
└─xvda1   202:1    0   8G  0 part /
xvdb      202:16   0  20G  0 disk


[root@ip-10-203-10-99 ~]# e2fsck -f /dev/xvdb
e2fsck 1.42.9 (28-Dec-2013)
Pass 1: Checking inodes, blocks, and sizes
Pass 2: Checking directory structure
Pass 3: Checking directory connectivity
Pass 4: Checking reference counts
Pass 5: Checking group summary information
/dev/xvdb: 13/1310720 files (7.7% non-contiguous), 215923/5242880 blocks


[root@ip-10-203-10-99 ~]# resize2fs /dev/xvdb
resize2fs 1.42.9 (28-Dec-2013)
Resizing the filesystem on /dev/xvdb to 7864320 (4k) blocks.
The filesystem on /dev/xvdb is now 7864320 blocks long.


[root@ip-10-203-10-99 ~]# mount -a


[root@ip-10-203-10-99 ~]# df -mh /opt/data
Filesystem       Size  Used Avail Use% Mounted on
/dev/xvdb         30G  394M   28G   2% /opt/data


[root@ip-10-203-10-99 ~]# ls -alh /opt/data
total 351M
drwxr-xr-x 3 root root 4.0K Nov  9 21:06 .
drwxr-xr-x 4 root root 4.0K Nov  9 21:03 ..
-rw-r--r-- 1 root root 250M Nov  9 21:05 test
```

Change volume from magnetic to SSD

One method to get some increased I/O performance is to change the volume from magnetic to a general purpose SSD, which has a throughput of about 128 MB/s. To do this, select the snapshot that we created for the volume, and click **Create Volume** from the **Actions** drop-down menu. Once this volume is available, attach it as /dev/ sdb to the instance. From the running instance we will mount it back, ensure that no loss of data has occurred, and check for an increase in throughput:

```
[root@ip-10-203-10-99 ~]# mount -a

[root@ip-10-203-10-99 ~]# ls /opt/data
lost+found  test

[root@ip-10-203-10-99 ~]# time dd if=/dev/zero of=/opt/data/test1 bs=512k
count=200
200+0 records in
200+0 records out
104857600 bytes (105 MB) copied, 1.5918 s, 65.9 MB/s

real    0m1.600s
user    0m0.008s
sys     0m0.068s
```

Here, we can see that we nearly doubled our throughput.

Increase I/O through software RAID

 If you wish to read more about the different software RAID levels and how they perform in the AWS virtualized environment, more information can be found at their User Guide at http://docs.aws. amazon.com/AWSEC2/latest/UserGuide/raid-config.html.

As seen, the throughput for the new file was about 1.6 GB/s for creation and about 40 MB/s for a rewrite. Magnetic EBS volumes are estimated between 40 and 90 MB/s. This is a very rough estimation, but will help to show even the most basic improvement of throughput. What we will do now is change the 20 GB magnetic drive into a software defined RAID0 drive, without losing any data. We cannot simply create a RAID device from a single snapshot, since the snapshot that we created was for a non-RAID ext4 filesystem. What we will do instead, is add two additional volumes to the host, configure them as RAID, and then move the data from one drive to another.

First we will create two new magnetic drives of 10 GB and attach them to the instance as /dev/sdc and /dev/sdd respectively. Once they are attached, we will format them and set them up from the instance into a software RAID0 configuration:

```
[root@ip-10-203-10-99 ~]# lsblk
NAME      MAJ:MIN RM SIZE RO TYPE MOUNTPOINT
xvda      202:0    0  8G  0 disk
└─xvda1 202:1    0  8G  0 part /
xvdb      202:16   0 20G  0 disk /opt/data
xvdc      202:32   0 10G  0 disk
xvdd      202:48   0 10G  0 disk


[root@ip-10-203-10-99 ~]# mdadm --create --verbose /dev/md0
--level=stripe --raid-devices=2 /dev/xvdc /dev/xvdd
mdadm: chunk size defaults to 512K
mdadm: Defaulting to version 1.2 metadata
mdadm: array /dev/md0 started.


[root@ip-10-203-10-99 ~]# mkfs.ext4 /dev/md0
mke2fs 1.42.9 (28-Dec-2013)
Filesystem label=
OS type: Linux
Block size=4096 (log=2)
Fragment size=4096 (log=2)
Stride=128 blocks, Stripe width=256 blocks
1310720 inodes, 5242624 blocks
262131 blocks (5.00%) reserved for the super user
First data block=0
Maximum filesystem blocks=2153775104
160 block groups
32768 blocks per group, 32768 fragments per group
8192 inodes per group
Superblock backups stored on blocks:
        32768, 98304, 163840, 229376, 294912, 819200, 884736, 1605632,
2654208,
        4096000


Allocating group tables: done
Writing inode tables: done
Creating journal (32768 blocks): done
```

```
Writing superblocks and filesystem accounting information: done

[root@ip-10-203-10-99 ~]# mkdir /opt/newdata

[root@ip-10-203-10-99 ~]# sed -i.bak '$ d' /etc/fstab #rm old drive mount

[root@ip-10-203-10-99 ~]# echo $'/dev/md0\t/opt/data\text4\
tdefaults,nofail\t0\t2'  >> /etc/fstab

[root@ip-10-203-10-99 ~]# mount /dev/md0 /opt/newdata

[root@ip-10-203-10-99 ~]# cp -r /opt/data/* /opt/newdata/

[root@ip-10-203-10-99 ~]# ls /opt/newdata/
lost+found   test

[root@ip-10-203-10-99 ~]# umount /opt/data /opt/newdata && rm -rf /opt/
newdata/ && mount -a

[root@ip-10-203-10-99 ~]# time dd if=/dev/zero of=/opt/data/test1 bs=512k
count=200
200+0 records in
200+0 records out
104857600 bytes (105 MB) copied, 0.0663928 s, 1.6 GB/s

real    0m0.067s
user    0m0.000s
sys     0m0.064s

[root@ip-10-203-10-99 ~]# time dd if=/dev/zero of=/opt/data/test1 bs=512k
count=200
200+0 records in
200+0 records out
104857600 bytes (105 MB) copied, 1.71824 s, 61.0 MB/s

real    0m1.729s
user    0m0.000s
sys     0m0.076s
```

As seen here, we increased the throughput to nearly double by utilizing software level RAID0 over a single magnetic volume.

Summary

In this chapter, we went through some very basic Cloud patterns for instance resiliency. We covered how to make volume level backups of volumes, to help guard against data loss across availability zone failures. We also covered how to create base AMIs, which can be reused as stamps. We touched upon some examples of scaling up by increasing virtual machine hardware specs, and how to scale horizontally using instance alarms and auto scaling groups. Lastly, we covered how to improve performance and modify the size of instance volumes without shutting down the running instance.

In the next chapter, we will cover some more complicated patterns aimed towards highly-available applications, or applications that cannot have downtime.

3

Patterns for High Availability

A very important topic, for most operations teams, is how to keep the systems responsive. Many things can cause an application to behave improperly with the end user, and there are a lot of different methods to handle these issues. The types of preventive measures used depend heavily on the purpose of that application in the system. Many applications are moving towards a microservice approach, in which the system is divided into smaller subsystems that have one task. This microservice approach is similar to software development life cycles, in which large sections of code are divided into smaller sections. This breaking up of responsibilities makes testing them a bit simpler in that each subsystem has a very specific and predictable job. Another benefit from an operational standpoint is that the system can be scaled horizontally, depending on which part is the bottleneck.

Breaking up the application into scalable pieces creates an issue. Similarly, there are many other issues that might arise for the operations team to handle. As stated in the introductory chapter, IaaS is great in that it leverages a lot of abstractions to the core hardware itself, to allow unique solutions to common problems. Although the hardware is abstracted away, it is in no way a perfect system, and can cause problems to the systems and applications within the infrastructure itself.

Power outages, hardware failures, and data center upgrades are just a few of the many problems that will still bubble up to the teams responsible for the systems. Data center upgrades are common, and given enough time at AWS, any team will get an e-mail or notification stating that some servers will shut down, or experience brownouts, or small outages of power. The best way to handle these is to span across data centers so that, if a single location experiences issues, the systems will continue to respond.

Multi-server pattern

Consider a two-tier architecture in which there is a **User Interface (UI)** instance that connects to a database instance. Now suppose that the system gets a large burst of traffic. Using the scale out pattern discussed in *Chapter 2, Basic Patterns*, the operations team can manually or automatically add more UI instances to the load balancer to mitigate the flux in traffic. This server redundancy pattern is the multi-server pattern. This pattern includes a healthcheck on the instance so that, if one of the instances that the load is being distributed across is misbehaving, it will not continue to route into it.

 One might note that this pattern is similar to the scale out pattern except that it is not dynamic in nature. In this pattern, we are discussing the details of adding horizontal scalability in a much simpler example.

A few things should be noted before we continue, however. It has been found, in my personal usage as well as documented cases, that the servers should be configured in an *N+1* configuration. If a single front-end is acceptable, then it should be configured for two. This allows for hiccups and brown-outs, as well as an influx of traffic into the system with minimal effect to the end users.

Lastly, be very careful when it comes to servers that contain session data or data of any kind. If it is a UI that requires sessions, it should be configured for an external session manager, such as the AWS-provided ElastiCache. If the system is responsible for data, such as a database, it should be configured for data replication and sharing, such as enterprise clustering. These are not covered in this pattern.

 For more information on ElastiCache visit `http://aws.amazon.com/elasticache`.

In this example, we will cover how to add a bit of redundancy and processing power through multiple instances using a load balancer. The general workflow will be as follows:

- Create an EC2 instance that services HTTP content
- Create an ELB that services traffic to the EC2 instance
- Clone the EC2 instance via the stamp pattern
- Add the newly created instance to the ELB

First, let's configure a Linux server from the AWS Linux AMI to serve some static
HTTP content. Launch an instance from the AWS EC2 console based on the AWS
Linux AMI, as per your environment. Once it is running, we will SSH into it and
configure it to be an HTTP server.

```
marc-win8:~ $ ssh -i ~/.ssh/mykey.pem ec2-user@10.203.10.191
The authenticity of host '10.203.10.191 (10.203.10.191)' can't be established.
ECDSA key fingerprint is d4:a7:5a:99:5b:6c:67:1f:f1:9b:53:05:4d:b6:39:58.
Are you sure you want to continue connecting (yes/no)? yes
Warning: Permanently added '10.203.10.191' (ECDSA) to the list of known hosts.

       _|  _|_ )
      _|  (    /   Amazon Linux AMI
     _|\___|___|

https://aws.amazon.com/amazon-linux-ami/2014.09-release-notes/
10 package(s) needed for security, out of 24 available
Run "sudo yum update" to apply all updates.
[ec2-user@ip-10-203-10-191 ~]$ sudo su -
[root@ip-10-203-10-191 ~]# yum install -y httpd >/dev/null 2>&1
[root@ip-10-203-10-191 ~]# echo 'welcome' > /var/www/html/index.html
[root@ip-10-203-10-191 ~]# service httpd start; chkconfig httpd on
Starting httpd: httpd: apr_sockaddr_info_get() failed for ip-10-203-10-191
httpd: Could not reliably determine the server's fully qualified domain name, using 127.0.0.1 for ServerName
                                                           [  OK  ]
[root@ip-10-203-10-191 ~]#
```

Now that it is an HTTP server that listens on port 80, we will create a new load
balancer for this instance. From the AWS EC2 console, select **Load Balancers** under
NETWORK & SECURITY.

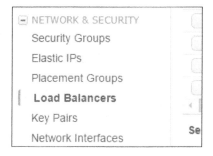

Create a new load balancer by selecting the **Create Load Balancer** option. At the **Define Load Balancer** tab, configure it as per your environment, ensuring that it has a listener for port 80 via HTTP. Click **Continue**.

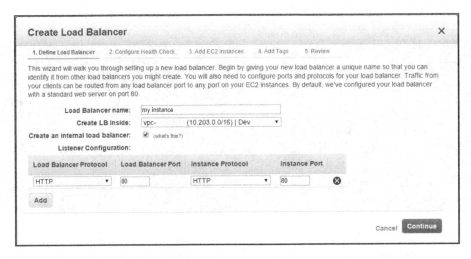

On the **Configure Health Check** tab, create a health check for port 80 via HTTP to '/'.

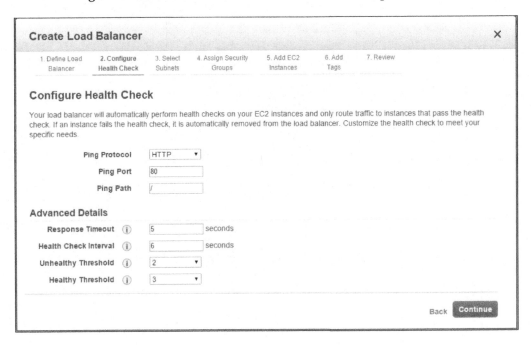

Continue with any options that pertain to your environment for both **Select Subnets** and the **Assign Security Groups** tabs. Then click **Continue**. At the **Add EC2 Instances** tab, assign the instance that we configured previously and click **Continue** as shown in the following screenshot:

Continue with any options that pertain to your environment for the **Add Tags** tab and click **Continue**. Lastly, click **Create** on the **Review** tab to create the load balancer. You will then be greeted with the success prompt, which you can close.

Select the load balancer you created in the list and select the **Instances** tab to see the status of the instances that are assigned to the load balancer. Once the **Status** shows **InService,** as shown in the following screenshot, we are ready to move on:

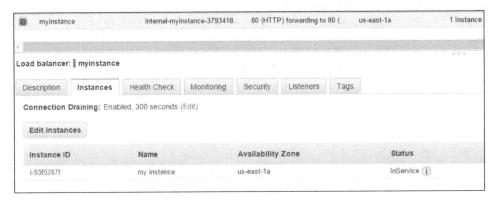

Select the instance ID for the only instance in the load balancer, under the **Instance ID** column. From here, create an AMI of the instance as described in the *Stamp pattern* section from *Chapter 2, Basic Patterns*. Once the AMI is complete and shows **available** in the **Status** column of the AMI's section of the EC2 console, select **Launch** and follow the steps from the stamp pattern to launch a new instance from this AMI.

Once complete, navigate back to the load balancer shown in the preceding screenshot by clicking **Load Balancers** under **NETWORK & SECURITY**. Select the load balancer you created in the list and select the **Instances** tab. Select **Edit Instances** on this tab.

At the **Add and Remove Instances** prompt, add the new instance that we just created and click **Save**.

 A periodic manual refresh of the page may be required to display the change in **Status**.

Wait until the **Status** shows **InService** for both instances as indicated in the following screenshot:

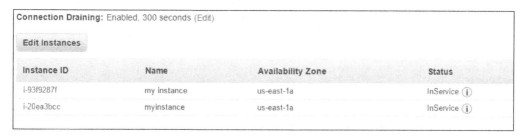

If you were to watch the requests for both the instances and issue requests to the load balancer, you would see that it is equally distributed across both. There is more to the load balancing algorithm than round-robin but that will not be discussed in detail here. What we have done, however, is added some resiliency to the servers in that, if one were to go down, the other would still be able to serve requests to the end user.

More information on the specifics of the load balancing algorithm used for AWS Elastic load balancers can be found at `http://docs.aws.amazon.com/ElasticLoadBalancing/latest/DeveloperGuide/TerminologyandKeyConcepts.html`.

Let's see what happens when we cause an instance to fail a health check. SSH into any of the two instances configured in the load balancer and run the following code:

```
[ec2-user@ip-10-203-10-191 ~]$ sudo service httpd stop
Stopping httpd:                                            [  OK  ]
[ec2-user@ip-10-203-10-191 ~]$
```

If you refresh the **Instances** tab of the load balancer (the amount of time is determined by the health check), you will notice that the instance we just stopped, that is, the `httpd` service, for now shows **OutOfService** for its **Status** column, as expected.

Edit Instances			
Instance ID	Name	Availability Zone	Status
i-93f9287f	my instance	us-east-1a	OutOfService ⓘ
i-20ea3bcc	myinstance	us-east-1a	InService ⓘ

If you issue a request to the load balancer, it will continue to respond as though nothing has happened. This completes the multi-server pattern.

```
Marc-win8:~ $ curl internal-myinstance-37934186.us-east-1.elb.amazonaws.com
welcome
```

Multi-data center pattern

The multi-server pattern guarantees resiliency at the server level, but can introduce an edge case. If the data center that the UI instances are in, goes under maintenance or has hardware failures that propagate upwards to the instances themselves, they might affect the end users, which is not acceptable. The UI instances cannot or should not be clustered, but should be present across different availability zones. This spanning across availability zones presents datacenter redundancy and is presented in the multi-data center pattern.

The steps for this pattern are nearly identical to the steps in the previous pattern except for two key differences. The first key difference is that the load balancer itself must cross multiple availability zones through subnets.

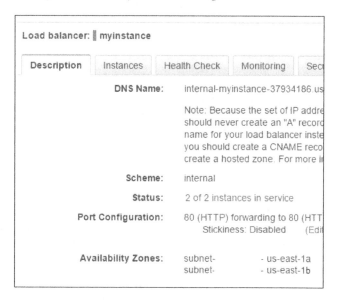

The other key difference is that the instances attached to the load balancer should be in different availability zones. Since the load balancer is in two zones, the instances should be in each zone as well.

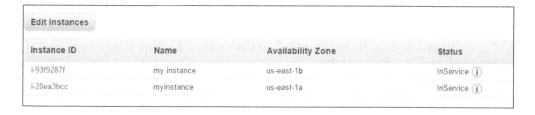

The ELB is a highly available AWS-provided service and is protected against terminations. This means that if a data center goes into maintenance mode, or has hardware failures, the end users will not experience any downtime. It is important to know that any databases that are not controlled by AWS services might take additional work to cross availability zones, such as clustering, to slave nodes that are in a different zone.

Floating IP pattern

Another set of issues to tackle is that of a system without a load balancer. Suppose a single server exists with an external IP address to reach it. A new set of patches have come out, or a new release to the operating system core is required. The instance cannot stop responding to the external users or systems communicating with the instance, so the patches cannot be made in-place.

A traditional way to resolve this might be to change the DNS entry to a temporary instance that is not being upgraded. But this might cause issues if the external systems do not use the DNS entry, or have cached it and try to continue to talk to the instance being modified. The pattern that can be used to mitigate this is the floating IP pattern. In this pattern, an **Elastic IP (EIP)** is used and is assigned to the original server to be modified.

When the modifications are required, the instance is cloned using the stamp pattern and the EIP is assigned to that instance. This EIP is immediate and does not affect DNS or any instances that might use DNS lookups during this time. When the modifications are complete, the EIP can be configured back to the original instance.

The general workflow of this pattern will be:

- Create an EC2 instance that serves HTTP content to an end user
- Assign a floating IP address to the EC2 instance
- Create a secondary EC2 instance that serves HTTP content to the end users
- Swap the floating IP address to the secondary EC2 instance
- Perform modifications to the original EC2 instance
- Swap the floating IP address back to the original EC2 instance once modifications are complete

First, we will launch a new instance of the AWS Linux AMI. Follow the traditional steps for launching an instance for your environment. Once it is complete, we will configure it to have an Elastic IP. From the AWS EC2 console, select **Elastic IPs** under **NETWORK & SECURITY**. From this new frame, select **Allocate New Address**.

At the **Allocate New Address** prompt, make no changes and select **Yes, Allocate**.

A new Elastic IP will be created for you and added to the list. Select it and click **Associate Address**.

At the **Associate Address** prompt, find your instance either by its **Instance ID,** or by searching its name in the **Instance** field. Then click **Associate**.

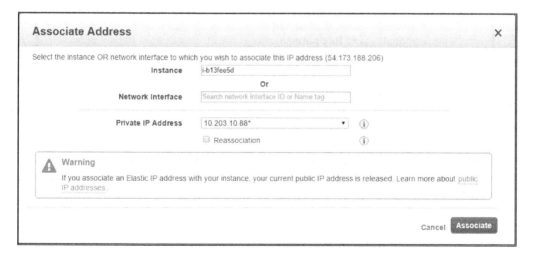

We will not configure the instance as shown in the next screenshot:

```
                                                          Cmder
arc-wine:~ $ ssh -i ~/.ssh/mykey.pem ec2-user@10.203.10.191
The authenticity of host '10.203.10.191 (10.203.10.191)' can't be established.
ECDSA key fingerprint is d4:a7:5a:99:5b:6c:67:1f:f1:9b:53:05:4d:b6:39:58.
Are you sure you want to continue connecting (yes/no)? yes
warning: Permanently added '10.203.10.191' (ECDSA) to the list of known hosts.

       _|  _|_  )
     _|  (      /      Amazon Linux AMI
      _|\___|___|

https://aws.amazon.com/amazon-linux-ami/2014.09-release-notes/
10 package(s) needed for security, out of 24 available
Run "sudo yum update" to apply all updates.
[ec2-user@ip-10-203-10-191 ~]$ sudo su -
[root@ip-10-203-10-191 ~]# yum install -y httpd >/dev/null 2>&1
[root@ip-10-203-10-191 ~]# echo 'welcome' > /var/www/html/index.html
[root@ip-10-203-10-191 ~]# service httpd start; chkconfig httpd on
Starting httpd: httpd: apr_sockaddr_info_get() failed for ip-10-203-10-191
httpd: Could not reliably determine the server's fully qualified domain name, using 127.0.0.1 for ServerName
                                                         [  OK  ]
[root@ip-10-203-10-191 ~]#
```

If you were to test the Elastic IP we just associated, using the following code, it should perform as expected. Note that the server responds from Apache 2.2.8, as it will be useful later:

```
$ curl http://54.173.188.206
welcome
$ curl -v http://54.173.188.206 2>&1 | grep \<\ Server:
< Server: Apache/2.2.28 (Amazon)
```

> It should be noted that if the instance being modified contained any kind of session data for the end user, they may experience some side effects, such as having to log in again, and so on. This is not relevant to the current scenario but might be relevant in applications of this pattern.

From the AWS EC2 console, create an AMI of the instance, as described in the *Stamp pattern* section from *Chapter 2, Basic Patterns*. Once the AMI is complete and shows **available** in the **Status** column of the AMI's section of the EC2 console, select **Launch** and follow the steps from the stamp pattern to launch a new instance from this AMI.

Once this instance is running, we will release the Elastic IP from the current instance and assign it to the new instance. From the AWS EC2 console, select **Elastic IPs** under **NETWORK & SECURITY**. From this new frame, select the Elastic IP that we configured earlier and select **Disassociate Address**. Next select **Yes, Disassociate** when prompted.

Now that it is no longer associated with any instances, we will associate it with the new instance that we created from the AMI. With the same Elastic IP still selected, click **Associate Address**.

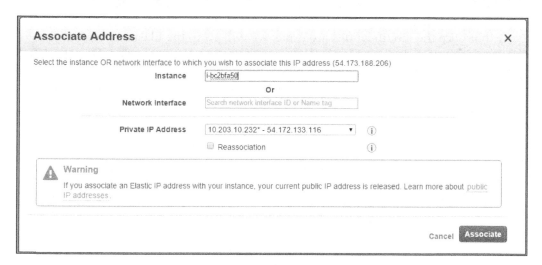

We are now free to modify the original instance as needed, without worry to the end user. As they continue to use the Elastic IP, we configured a DNS entry that points to the Elastic IP and the end user will continue to get a response without any worry of cache. This is transparent to the user. We will now make modifications to the original server as shown in the next screenshot:

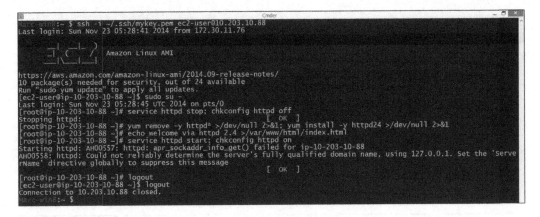

Now that once the modifications are done, we will swap the Elastic IP back to the original instance. Select the Elastic IP we configured earlier, and select **Disassociate Address**. Select **Yes, Disassociate** when prompted. Now, choose the original Elastic IP and click **Associate Address**. From the **Associate Address** prompt, find your instance either by its `Instance ID`, or by searching its name in the **Instance** field. Click on **Associate**.

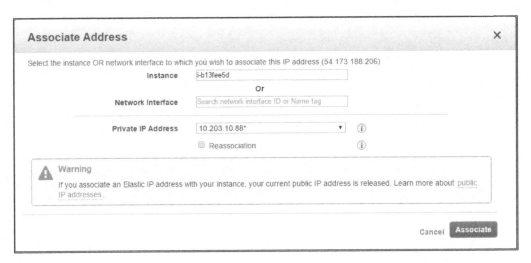

If we try to hit the Elastic IP, we will get the information from the server after modifications were made. Originally it responded with `welcome` from `Apache 2.2.29`. We will prove now that it returns the new body from `Apache 2.4`:

```
$ curl --silent -v http://54.173.188.206 2>&1 | grep \<\ Server:
< Server: Apache/2.4.10 (Amazon)
$ curl http://54.173.188.206
welcome via httpd 2.4
```

We successfully used an Elastic IP to swap instances with minimal downtime to the end user so that completes the floating IP pattern. A useful note to make is that Elastic IPs are per-account and can be used regardless of availability zone.

> While the high availability patterns aim for zero-downtime, it should be noted that this pattern does introduce a small window of downtime. The reason this pattern still falls under the category, however, is because the window of connectivity is much lower than that of a DNS change, which is a typical solution to server swapping, without using any external services.

Deep health check pattern

Let's consider an example using the two-tier architecture again. So far we have shown how to replicate the UI across single and multiple availability zones, through the multi-server and multi-data center patterns. These patterns used a health check on the server itself to let the load balancer know that the server is operational. The thing that is missing from this is a health check that lets the load balancer know that the database is operational.

The deep health check pattern lets the instances connected to the load balancer, or in this case the UI instances, notify the load balancer of health checks beyond the grasp of the load balancer itself. The example that we will discuss will use a page from the UI instance to return either a `200 OK` response or a `500 Internal Server Error` if the database is having issues.

The database in this example has no way of letting the load balancer know whether it is in a healthy state. The way we will get to this information is to create a route in the UI instance that tries to connect to the database and returns the response code based on if it can, or cannot connect.

It is important to note that this does not provide high availability like the other patterns because there is no way to repair the database in the example, which we will go through.

In the real-world, the database would be a master-slave configuration across availability zones and the UI instances would not report back whether it could, or could not connect because no action from them or the load balancer would be required. This is because failover should be built into the clustering configuration of the database itself.

Some other real-life use-cases would be similar in that deep health checks would be configured, but would not report them directly to the load balancer. For example, imagine the system has a service that interacts with a queue. If the response time of the queue reached a threshold, or the queue reached a great depth, it would report an alarm. Alarms allow auto scaling groups to scale both up and down, based on the alarm triggered. That is beyond the reach of this example.

The general workflow for this pattern will be:

- Create a load balancer that determines overall health by using the PHP webpage provided by the EC2 web instance
- Create a database instance that contains a very small subset of data
- Create an EC2 instance that has a PHP webpage that reports the status code to a database instance

First, we will configure a load balancer similar to the others with no instances. Make sure the load balancer has a health check for /dbcheck.php. Once complete, we will configure a MySQL database server. Launch an instance from the AWS Linux AMI based on your configuration and SSH into it when it is ready:

```
[ec2-user@ip-10-203-10-174 ~]$ sudo su -
[root@ip-10-203-10-174 ~]# yum groupinstall -y "MySQL Database" >/dev/
null 2>&1
[root@ip-10-203-10-174 ~]# service mysqld start; chkconfig mysqld on
                                                        [  OK  ]
Starting mysqld:                                        [  OK  ]
[root@ip-10-203-10-174 ~]# /usr/bin/mysqladmin -u root password 'Abc1234'
[root@ip-10-203-10-174 ~]# mysql -uroot -pAbc1234 <<EOF
> create database foo;
> create table blah (
> id INT AUTO_INCREMENT PRIMARY KEY,
> text varchar(20)
> );
> insert into blah set text='wat';
> select * from blah
```

```
> EOF
+----+------+
| id | text |
+----+------+
|  1 | wat  |
+----+------+
[root@ip-10-203-10-174 ~]# mysql -uroot -pAbc1234 <<EOF
> GRANT ALL PRIVILEGES ON *.* TO 'root'@'%' IDENTIFIED BY 'Abc1234';
> FLUSH PRIVILEGES;
> EOF
```

Next we will configure a UI instance that uses PHP5 and has a route /dbcheck that returns a response code based on whether it could, or could not connect to the database. Launch a new instance from the AWS Linux AMI and SSH into it when it is ready.

 Please note that the code is not usable as it is, and might require modifications to sections in bold.

```
[ec2-user@ip-10-203-10-154 ~]$ sudo su -
[root@ip-10-203-10-154 ~]# yum groupinstall -y "Web Server" "PHP
Support" >/dev/null 2>&1
[root@ip-10-203-10-154 ~]# yum install -y php php-mysql >/dev/null
2>&1
[root@ip-10-203-10-154 ~]# service httpd start; chkconfig httpd on
 Starting httpd: httpd: apr_sockaddr_info_get() failed for ip-10-203-
10-154
httpd: Could not reliably determine the server's fully qualified
domain name, using 127.0.0.1 for ServerName
                                                          [  OK  ]
[root@ip-10-203-10-154 ~]# groupadd www; usermod -a -G www ec2-user;
chown -R root:www /var/www
[root@ip-10-203-10-154 ~]# chmod 2775 /var/www
[root@ip-10-203-10-154 ~]# find /var/www -type d -exec sudo chmod 2775
{} +; find /var/www -type f -exec sudo chmod 0664 {} +
[root@ip-10-203-10-154 ~]# su ec2-user -c 'echo "<?php phpinfo(); ?>"
> /var/www/html/phpinfo.php'
[root@ip-10-203-10-154 ~]# cat <<EOF >/var/www/html/dbcheck.php
 <?php
\$servername = "DB_INSTANCE_ID";
```

```
\$username = "root";
\$password = "Abc1234";

// Create connection
\$conn = new mysqli(\$servername, \$username, \$password);

// Check connection
if (\$conn->connect_error) {
    header('HTTP/1.1 500 Internal Server Error');
    die("Connection failed: " . \$conn->connect_error);
}
echo "Connected successfully";
?>
EOF
[root@ip-10-203-10-154 ~]# curl --silent -sL -w "%{http_code}\\n"
"http://localhost/dbcheck.php" -o /dev/null
200
```

From the AWS EC2 console, select **Load Balancers** under **NETWORK & SECURITY**.
Select the load balancer you created in the list and select the **Instances** tab to see the
status of the instances that are assigned to the load balancer. Click **Edit Instances,**
and add the EC2 instance that hosts the PHP web application. Now click **Save**. Once
the **Status** shows **InService** as shown in the following screenshot, we are ready to
move on.

[Please note that you may have to periodically refresh the page
manually, to see a change in **Status**.]

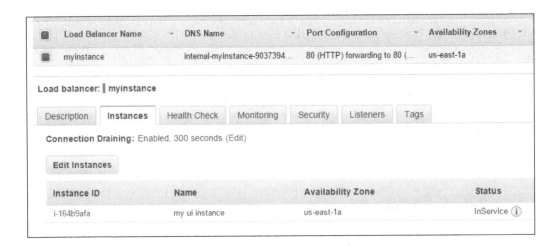

What this means is that our deep health check is working successfully. The load balancer is consistently getting a valid response from the pass-through URI, from the UI instance via the dbcheck.php page provided. To verify whether this is working as expected, we should break it. SSH back into the DB instance and stop the database service.

Back to the load balancer in just a moment or two, the service should change to **OutOfService** since the database is no longer connectable.

Instance ID	Name	Availability Zone	Status
i-164b9afa	my ui instance	us-east-1a	OutOfService ⓘ

This concludes the deep health check pattern.

Summary

In this chapter, we discussed a topic that helps to reduce downtime during planned operational windows, such as the Elastic IP pattern. We also discussed a few patterns that help to make resilient server architectures, such as the multi-server pattern, which helps to maintain servers over general failures and traffic spikes, as well as the multi-data center pattern, which helps to create more resilient tiers that can withstand availability zone outages. The last pattern that we discussed is the deep health pattern, which aims to change the thought process on how to handle architectures where servers cannot be reached from the load balancers themselves.

In the upcoming chapter we will discuss patterns to process static data.

4
Patterns for Processing Static Data

A common topic that everyone in technology comes across is **static data**. Static data is just that: data that doesn't change. Some examples of static data would be HTML web pages with CSS and JavaScript, XML, binary files, and so on. When it comes to this type of data, the common issue that arises out of operations or development is what to do with it to get it to the end user.

Since this book is aimed at Cloud infrastructure and has been heavily tied to web applications, it might be obvious that the static data we will use throughout the examples will be binary data and static HTML. Let's suppose you have some static web pages such as documentation that needs to be accessible to an end user. We could easily just create a virtual machine to host it using Nginx or Apache but we are stuck again with having to solve redundancy, fail over, and high availability.

Instead of creating a virtual machine, load balancers, backup policies, and causing more headaches, what if we could leverage the services provided by AWS, which give us all of the benefits of high availability and resiliency out of the box? The topics covered in this chapter will give a few different approaches to doing just this.

Some of the patterns that we will cover in this chapter are as follows:

- High availability storage pattern
- Direct storage hosting pattern
- Private data delivery pattern
- Content delivery networks pattern
- Rename distribution pattern

High availability storage

Let's suppose we have a site, dynamic or static, that serves large files such as video files. The best approach to handling this situation would be to host the web server, as any web application with the HTTP server serving the HTML content directly will not have the large files on the server itself.

With this method, we could use any deployment method for getting the code from source control into the server and not have to worry about maintaining the other files. Failover on the instance can be taken care of as it would for any instance, through load balancers and auto scaling groups. Redundancy of the files outside of source control might be controlled through an AWS-provided service such as S3. Remember that with S3, redundancy, encryption, and failover are taken care of with no intervention or set up required.

As a bit of coverage, let's discuss S3 a bit more in detail. AWS' **Simple Storage Service** provides an unlimited amount of object storage. The root storage node for S3 is called a bucket, which has a unique identifier, and can have very specific access and control policies attached to it through IAM roles and bucket policies. Buckets can also be served directly as a static website through the console.

 Security policies will not be discussed in detail in this book. Further reading can be found in the AWS developer documentation at http://docs.aws.amazon.com/AWSEC2/latest/UserGuide/iam-roles-for-amazon-ec2.html and http://docs.aws.amazon.com/AmazonS3/latest/dev/example-bucket-policies.html.

Let's see what this would actually look like. The general workflow for this pattern will be as follows:

- Create a file and archive it into a zip folder on your local machine
- Upload the zipped file to a unique bucket in S3
- Create a bucket policy that allows internet users to access and download our zipped file via a web link through S3 website hosting
- Create an instance that uses an Apache web server to host a link to our zipped file

We start by creating a local ZIP archive file on your computer named
`importantstuff.zip`. Next, browse to the **S3** section of the AWS console so that we
can create a bucket with a unique name. It is important to note that the bucket name
must be unique globally, and not just to the user account. From the S3 main console
page select **Create Bucket**.

From the **Create a Bucket** pop-up, provide the unique name for the **Bucket Name**
and select a **Region** that makes sense for your environment. Then click **Create**.
When selecting the region there is no correct choice, but it should be chosen to be
geographically close to the end users. Since I am from the US, in this pattern, I select
the **US Standard** region.

While not the correct answer, the typical solution to creating unique
and readable S3 bucket names is to use the Java packaging standard
found on their documentation page at `http://docs.oracle.`
`com/javase/tutorial/java/package/namingpkgs.html`.

When the prompt closes, you will be left with the properties for the bucket on the right half of the AWS console. Expand the **Static Website Hosting** drop-down and select the **Enable website hosting** radio button. Provide `index.html` for the **Index Document** text field and `error.html` for the **Error Document** text field as seen in the next screenshot:

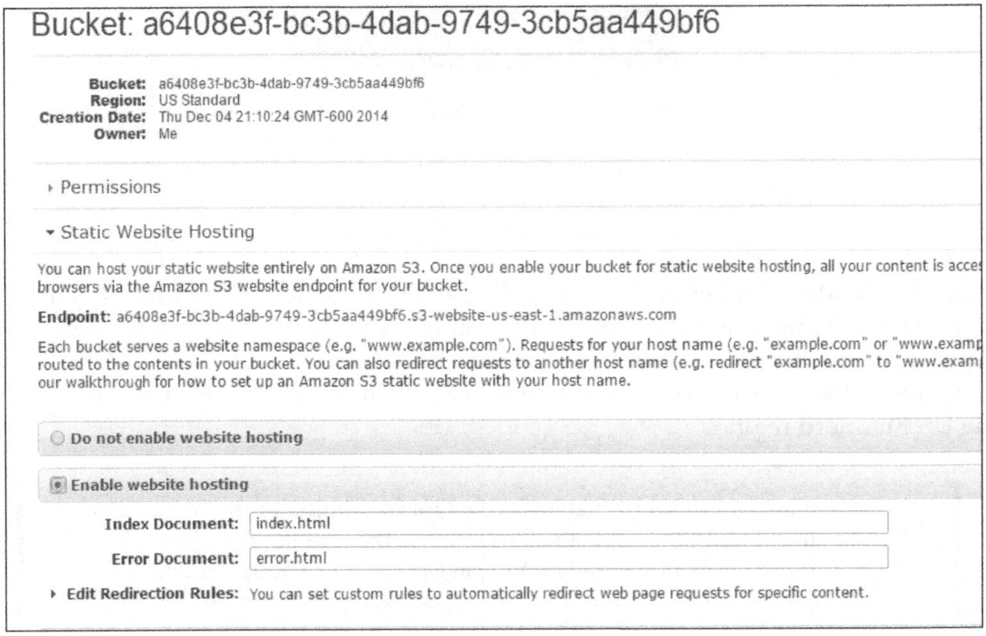

Now browse into the bucket we created by selecting it from the S3 console. Click the **Upload** button and drag the ZIP file, which we created in the beginning, here. Once it is prepared and listed in the upload list, select **Start Upload**.

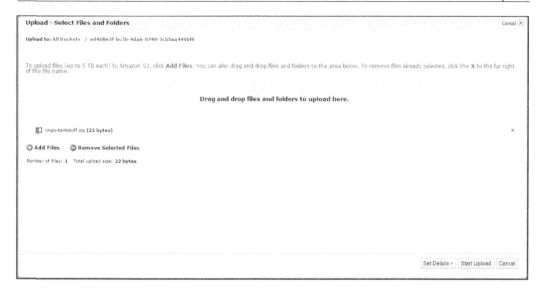

The ZIP archive will now upload and become available via S3 to anyone authorized to retrieve it. It is important to note that we have not modified permissions of the bucket at all, so if you try to retrieve this file from a web browser using the URL given by S3, you will get a **403 Forbidden error code**.

403 Forbidden

- Code: AccessDenied
- Message: Access Denied
- RequestId: C9330FEAAA5A3196
- HostId: xyuAuw4F+hD2N5P96ebsMomikgXoC2X00z+zR1u1CE8hpeAXaxXF0EtKxjI6tfASRb84lJVa7OE=

An Error Occurred While Attempting to Retrieve a Custom Error Document

- Code: AccessDenied
- Message: Access Denied

As stated earlier, we will not cover permissions for S3 in detail, but out of the box an S3 bucket only has permissions for the root account owner. If we wished to provide access to this bucket to certain users, profiles, groups, services, or accounts, we would configure IAM profiles for this bucket. For this example, we will open up this bucket via HTTP to anyone on the internet, and we will use a bucket policy to do this.

Back in the S3 console select the magnifying glass icon next to the bucket, to bring back the configuration properties for the bucket to the right of the console.

Expand the **Permission** drop-down, and select the **Add Bucket Policy** icon.

Bucket: a6408e3f-bc3b-4dab-9749-3cb5aa449bf6

Bucket: a6408e3f-bc3b-4dab-9749-3cb5aa449bf6
Region: US Standard
Creation Date: Thu Dec 04 21:10:24 GMT-600 2014
Owner: Me

▾ Permissions

Grantee: [   ] ☑ List ☑ Upload/Delete ☑ View Permissions ☑ Edit Permissions

⊕ **Add more permissions**   ▦ **Add bucket policy**   ▦ **Add CORS Configuration**

You will use a policy similar to the following one but note that it references the bucket name that will be unique to the reader:

```
{
  "Version":"2012-10-17",
  "Statement":[{
  "Sid":"PublicReadGetObject",
      "Effect":"Allow",
    "Principal": "*",
      "Action":["s3:GetObject"],
      "Resource":["arn:aws:s3:::a6408e3f-bc3b-4dab-9749-3cb5aa449bf6/*"
      ]
```

```
        }
    ]
}
```

Note that within the policy, we use the unique **Amazon Resource Name** (**ARN**) for our bucket. If the bucket you create has a different name, you would need to modify the previous policy to reflect it.

Click **Save** followed by **Close** to verify and apply the policy to the bucket. If this was successful in trying to retrieve the ZIP archive that failed earlier with a **403** error code, the file will be downloaded now.

We will now create a virtual machine that hosts static HTML with a link to S3 for the ZIP file so that this non-site data is not on the machine. From the **EC2** portion of the AWS console, launch an instance from the AWS Linux AMI based on your configuration, and SSH into it when it is ready.

Note that the pieces in bold might require modifications to work with your setup:

```
[ec2-user@ip-10-203-10-139 ~]$ sudo su -

[root@ip-10-203-10-139 ~]# yum install -y httpd >/dev/null 2>&1

[root@ip-10-203-10-139 ~]# cat <<EOF > /var/www/html/index.html

<HTML>

   <HEAD><TITLE>Wat</TITLE></HEAD>

   <BODY>

    <H1>Hello World</H1>

    <A HREF="http://a6408e3f-bc3b-4dab-9749-3cb5aa449bf6.s3-website-us-
east-1.amazonaws.com/importantstuff.zip">my super important ZIP file</A>

   </BODY>

</HTML>

EOF

[root@ip-10-203-10-139 ~]# service httpd start

Starting httpd: httpd: apr_sockaddr_info_get() failed for ip-10-203-10-
139

httpd: Could not reliably determine the server's fully qualified domain
name, using 127.0.0.1 for ServerName

                                                          [  OK  ]
```

What we have done at this point now is configured a web server via HTTP that will host a link to a file in S3. We could use the previous patterns to make this web server instance resilient by using auto scaling groups, scaling policies, and load balancers, and not worry about the state of the ZIP archive, or any data that is not relevant to the web server itself, for that matter. If you browse to the web instance virtual machine we just created and click the link, you will download the file from S3.

Direct storage hosting

The example for the previous pattern was a hybrid of AWS services that used a virtual machine for the web application layer, and the highly available S3 storage for non-application static data. You most likely noticed a very large improvement that could have been made, that is, of not using a virtual machine to host the static application content, and instead use S3 throughout.

In the direct storage hosting pattern, this will be the case where we will not have a virtual machine at all, but will host the entire web application through S3. It is important to note that this pattern is only useful for static website content. S3 does not have an execution layer, so it does not allow server-side languages such as PHP. Another point to note is that although JavaScript can be executed in this pattern, as it is client-side JavaScript, any asynchronous calls that are made to retrieve data will likely not have the same DNS entry. If that is the case, you might be able to utilize JSONP to allow cross-domain data access.

 JSONP is a very detailed subject by itself and will thus not be covered in this book. More information about this concept and safe usage can be found at `http://json-p.org/`.

For this pattern, browse to the S3 console and create a bucket, the bucket policy, and website sharing configuration for that bucket similar to the preceding high availability storage pattern.

 You could also use the same bucket created in the previous example and add the HTML files in it to skip the creation of a new bucket.

In this example, however, do not upload a single ZIP archive, but a full HTML suite. An example might be to create an `index.html` file that contains the following code:

```
<!doctype html>
<html lang="en">
<head>
    <meta charset="utf-8" />
```

```
<title>Hello World</title>
<!-- CSS for presentation. -->
<style>
h1 { font-size: 14px; color: hotpink; }
button { color: red; }
</style>
</head>
<body>
<h1>Hello World</h1>
<button>Click Me!</button>
<!-- JavaScript for interactivity. -->
<script>
// Get a handle on the first button element in the document.
var button = document.querySelector( "button" );
// If a user clicks on it, say hello!
button.addEventListener( "click", function( ev ) {
    alert( "Hello" );
}, false);

</script>
</body>
</html>
```

Next, browse to our bucket via a web browser and click the button to verify
our pattern.

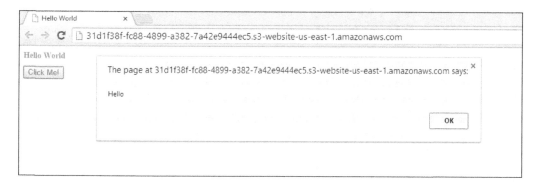

The previous code is a good example of using an HTML page with pure client-side
JavaScript to show what capabilities remain by using S3 as a web hosting platform.

Private data delivery

At this point in the chapter, we have covered two ways of delivering static content. The first was a pattern that lets us deploy a sort of hybrid service in which some files remain on S3, while the bulk of the application would reside on the server itself. In the second pattern, we discussed removing the hybrid portion and hosting all of this from within S3 without the need for a server.

While these previous examples solve a very simple problem, they might not solve a real-world issue such as securing data that does not reside on the server itself, similar to the hybrid high availability pattern. We should try to solve a real-world issue with a real code-based solution. Let's imagine that we have some large files in an S3 bucket that should not be publicly accessible by default.

Instead of just serving out the content to any connection, we should secure these files somehow. One approach might be to use policies on the bucket itself, but that requires maintaining a policy and knowledge of the files. In the private data delivery pattern, we will lock down the files with a time-sensitive URL that is native to the S3 API. We will implement a very simple login page through PHP and, if authorized, a URL will be generated to our file so that it can be reached.

First start an instance based on the AWS Linux AMI as per your environment configuration. Once it is running, SSH into it. Next, install Apache, as well as PHP and set permissions accordingly:

```
[ec2-user@ip-10-203-10-123 ~]$ sudo yum groupinstall -y "Web Server" "PHP
Support" >/dev/null 2>&1

[ec2-user@ip-10-203-10-123 ~]$ sudo chown -R ec2-user /var/www && sudo
chmod 2775 /var/www

[ec2-user@ip-10-203-10-123 ~]$ sudo su ec2-user -

[ec2-user@ip-10-203-10-123 ~]$ find /var/www -type d -exec sudo chmod
2775 {} + && find /var/www -type f -exec sudo chmod 0664 {} +

[ec2-user@ip-10-203-10-123 ~]$ sudo service httpd start >/dev/null 2>&1
```

What we have now is a valid PHP server, so let's create an `index.php` login page and a `register.php` page that handles hardcoded authorization, and generates a URL upon valid authorization:

```
[ec2-user@ip-10-203-10-123 ~]$ cat <<EOF >/var/www/html/index.php
<?xml version="1.0" encoding="UTF-8"?>
<html>
  <head>
    <title>login</title>
  </head>
```

```
    <body>
      <div class="register-form">
        <h1>Login</h1>
        <form action="register.php" method="POST">
          <p>
            <label>User Name : </label>
            <input id="username" type="text"
              name="username" placeholder="username" />
          </p>
          <p>
            <label>Password   : </label>
            <input id="password" type="password"
              name="password" placeholder="password" />
          </p>
          <a class="btn" href="register.php">Signup</a>
          <input class="btn register" type="submit"
            name="submit" value="Login" />
        </form>
      </div>
    </body>
</html>
EOF
[ec2-user@ip-10-203-10-123 ~]$ cat <<EOF >/var/www/html/register.php
 <?php  //Start the Session
    function el_crypto_hmacSHA1(\$key, \$data, \$blocksize = 64) {
        if (strlen(\$key) > \$blocksize) \$key = pack('H*',
sha1(\$key));
        \$key = str_pad(\$key, \$blocksize, chr(0x00));
        \$ipad = str_repeat(chr(0x36), \$blocksize);
        \$opad = str_repeat(chr(0x5c), \$blocksize);
        \$hmac = pack( 'H*', sha1(
        (\$key ^ \$opad) . pack( 'H*', sha1(
          (\$key ^ \$ipad) . \$data
        ))
      ));
    ));
    return base64_encode(\$hmac);
  }

  function el_s3_getTemporaryLink(\$accessKey, \$secretKey,
                                  \$bucket, \$path, \$expires = 5) {
    \$expires = time() + intval(floatval(\$expires) * 60);
    \$path = str_replace('%2F', '/',
                        rawurlencode(\$path = ltrim(\$path, '/')));
    \$signpath = '/'. \$bucket .'/'. \$path;
```

```
    \$signsz = implode("\n", \$pieces = array('GET', null, null,
                                        \$expires, \$signpath));
    \$signature = el_crypto_hmacSHA1(\$secretKey, \$signsz);
    \$url = sprintf('http://%s.s3.amazonaws.com/%s', \$bucket,
\$path);
    \$qs = http_build_query(\$pieces = array(
      'AWSAccessKeyId' => \$accessKey,
      'Expires' => \$expires,
      'Signature' => \$signature,
    ));
    return \$url.'?'.\$qs;
  }

  if (\$_POST['username'] == "admin" && \$_POST['password'] ==
"legit") {
    echo el_s3_getTemporaryLink('MY_ACCESS_KEY', 'MY_SECRET_KEY',
                              'a6408e3f-bc3b-4dab-9749-3cb5aa449bf6',
                              'importantstuff.zip');
  } else {
    header('Location: index.php');
  }
 ?>
EOF
```

The previous code requires a valid, environment-specific access key and secret key, as well as the S3 bucket name and filename for the ZIP archive.

What we have at this point, if you were to browse to the instance, is a web page that allows you to type in a username and password combination. Through that HTML form, it will pass the parameters to a validation page that looks for a hardcoded value, which if valid, will produce an S3 URL for our importantstuff.zip file with a time limit of five minutes. This means that any attempt at using the URL after the timeout will produce an HTTP 403 Unauthorized error code. The following code shows what that might look like.

Note that the IP address of the instance would need to be modified to the IP address of your instance.

```
[ec2-user@ip-10-203-10-123 ~]$ TEMP_URL=$(curl --silent -X POST -d
"username=admin&password=legit" http://10.203.10.123/register.php)
```

```
[ec2-user@ip-10-203-10-123 ~]$ curl -sL -w "%{http_code}\\n" $TEMP_URL
200
[ec2-user@ip-10-203-10-123 ~]$ sleep 301 && curl -sL -w "%{http_code}\\n"
$TEMP_URL
403
```

Content delivery networks

An issue that constantly arises with most operations teams is improving the user experience. There is no set-in-stone solution for this kind of optimization as it changes, based on countless variables. This book is mostly aimed at web applications, so one of the optimizations we could make in terms of static data could be by ensuring that this data does not have to travel very far to reach the end user. This, in turn, reduces latency to the user or the client system.

Content delivery networks aim to solve this very problem by ensuring that the data gets delivered to the user from a highly available server that is geographically nearest to them, or based on latency. AWS has a service called CloudFront, which aims to solve this very problem.

With CloudFront, an operations team could deploy servers on top of static content so that it is automatically cached and available to the end user in the best way possible, with very little work required to do so. In this example, we will serve out some static HTML content from an S3 bucket, launch a CloudFront distribution on top of that bucket, and then see what the latency looks like at two different locations in the world.

The first thing we should do is create an S3 bucket as in the previous examples. Again, we could reuse the buckets from the previous examples, if preferred. Once the bucket exists, ensure that it is serviced via HTTP using the Static Website Hosting service for the S3 bucket. Lastly, ensure that a bucket policy exists so that the content can be reached. See the attached code for an example of an HTML project. Once the S3 bucket contains the attached code, and can service it via a web browser, let's proceed by deploying a CloudFront edge server on this bucket.

From the AWS console, select **CloudFront** from the available services. From the CloudFront portion of the console, select **Create Distribution** from the available buttons.

From the **Select delivery method** frame, select **Get Started** under the **Web** option.

From the **Create distribution** frame, we can leave all defaults set except for **Origin Domain Name**, which should be set to the S3 bucket that we created and uploaded the static HTML into.

 It should be noted that the **Origin Domain Name** automatically lists and auto-completes with compatible bucket names (those that allow website hosting).

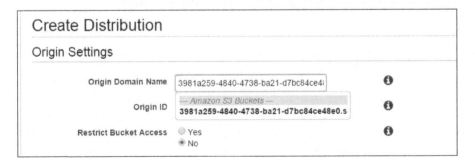

The last setting that should be set is the **Default Root Object** in the **Distribution Settings** section, which should be **index.html**.

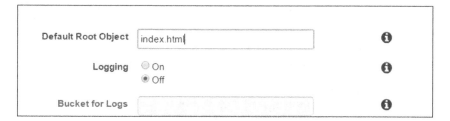

Finally, scroll to the bottom of this pane and select **Create Distribution** to finish the CloudFront edge server setup. This will take us back to the CloudFront distribution portion of the AWS CloudFront console. From here, the state of the server will stay as **In Progress** until the changes take effect across the servers around the world.

 It should be noted that this process can take up to 30 minutes to complete and might require manual refreshing to see a change in status.

Once the status changes to **Deployed,** we can now browse to it in a web browser by using the URL provided in the **Domain Name** column of the CloudFront console, to verify that things are working as expected.

Rename distribution pattern

The previous design pattern is a good example of distributing data across many servers through the CloudFront service. Static content is cached and serviced in an optimized manner so that the end user can have the best experience in retrieving pages and content. Underneath the covers, CloudFront caches the URL as a key so that if the URL is accessed again, it can be served immediately, or near-immediately.

Although static data is just that: static, it does not mean that it does not change. If the maintainer of the page decides to update any of the content, end users would still get the old data until the new changes have migrated across all edge servers. If there was a need to show new data without the worry of users seeing different pieces, a new method must be used.

As described previously, the URL of the pages and content are what is used in the cache. The best method for getting new data to the user is to lower the cache timeout in the created CloudFront distribution, as well as generating new URLs. Generating new URLs can be tricky without services such as URL shortening services such as `http://bit.ly` or `http://goo.gl`.

CloudFront servers with URL shortening, combined with the private data delivery pattern, is the best solution for delivery of static content with highly available non-application data.

Combining all of these concepts this way would allow you to generate signed, time sensitive (and short) URLs for the dynamic portions of the S3 objects (such as zipped files) while allowing the non-changing portions, such as the HTML content, to be cached. This allows for a robust end user experience, as well as a very resilient setup for the team managing the web application.

Assuming that the web application systems configured for the generation of signed URLs for S3 bucket data are configured across availability zones with a load balancer and auto scaling group configured for HTTP load, this three-tier configuration would provide a 100% scalable and redundant solution for static content.

Downloading the example code

You can download the example code files for all Packt books you have purchased from your account at `http://www.packtpub.com`. If you purchased this book elsewhere, you can visit `http://www.packtpub.com/support` and register to have the files e-mailed directly to you.

Summary

We covered a few methods of adding redundancy and optimization to static content in this chapter. The first three methods covered the AWS S3 service as a backend. The first pattern used S3 with an EC2 configured server to serve static application data from the server using S3 as a backend for non-application data. The next pattern covered using the S3 by itself as a web application server. The last of the S3-backed patterns used the AWS-provided URL generation API to generate time-limited URLs for S3-backed objects.

The last two patterns covered CloudFormation as a cache system to ensure that data was migrated to as many redundant servers as possible. The first pattern discussed the benefits of cache optimization, while the last one discussed how to tie all of these patterns together in a multi-tier, completely resilient static datastore.

In the next chapter we will shift our focus from static data to dynamic data.

5
Patterns for Processing Dynamic Data

In the previous chapter, we covered a few patterns that allow servers to offload static data, or data that does not require request-time parsing, to AWS-backed storage. This allowed us to take advantage of storage that required very little maintenance operationally and, instead, focus on optimization of delivery through cache, content delivery networks, and so on.

These previous patterns are very rarely encountered in real-world exercises, as static data is generally rare itself. Real-world web applications are, by design, dynamic for the data is not set in stone, but changes over time through usage. From here, many issues arise from having multiple servers attempting to share data that cannot be cached easily, or at all.

One of the worst things that could happen from an end user's perspective would be to visit a web application and get conflicting data each time they change pages, or even refresh. If the underlying systems cannot properly share the state or data, then it will become nearly unusable for any user that might try to utilize it.

Throughout this chapter, we will cover some patterns that help to mitigate the issues of data synchronization over complex systems, as well as attempting to cover how to scale up and out over data that is not static.

In this chapter we will cover the following topics:

- Clone server pattern
- NFS sharing pattern
- State sharing pattern
- URL rewriting pattern
- Cache proxy pattern

Clone server pattern

A common problem for any system administrator is keeping data persistent across servers. The approach for keeping data persistent across systems depends on the type of application, the filesystem used, and many other key factors. For example, a database would be clustered across multiple instances so that the data could be shared (or stored in separate blocks) in an optimal way, or so that indexes could be used properly for data in different locations.

The type of application we will cover in this example should be simple, so we will investigate how to scale horizontally using a simple HTTP server that allows for file uploads. In the previously touched scale out pattern, we covered how to create a server that hosts HTML content via Apache, and how to increase the throughput by cloning the server behind a load balancer. That example assumed no dynamic data because if anything were uploaded to the server, it would be lost when scaled down or not reachable, depending on which instance the load balancer chose for the user on the request. Each request would offer potentially different data to the end user, which could be quite frustrating.

The example covered here will expand the functionality by maintaining a master instance that will never be scaled out, and scaling up new instances that will copy data from the master instance on a timer to themselves. While this may not be a real-world example, it does cover some basic maneuvers on how to shift data between servers in real time.

There are some drawbacks to the example that we will cover. This would not work for complex systems, or systems with a lot of data since rsync will take a growing amount of time to complete as the amount of data grows. There is also very little error checking or validation among many other best-practice issues that should be avoided in production environments. Also, the example would not work for database instances where maintaining the files themselves is not enough to make the application usable. Lastly, in this example, the master instance becomes a single point of failure, as the data is not resilient against any kind of faults. That is, if the master instance failed, the slaves would not be able to copy new data to them or their siblings.

First, launch an instance as per your environment needs, based on the AWS Linux AMI. Once it is up and running, we will configure it to be an Apache HTTP server with PHP support, as well as put our base PHP files so that it becomes usable:

```
[ec2-user@ip-10-203-10-123 ~]$ sudo yum groupinstall -y "Web Server" "PHP
Support" >/dev/null 2>&1

[ec2-user@ip-10-203-10-123 ~]$ sudo usermod -aG apache ec2-user

[ec2-user@ip-10-203-10-123 ~]$ sudo su ec2-user - # refresh groups and
apply new apache group
```

```
[ec2-user@ip-10-203-10-123 ~]$ sudo chown -R root:apache /var/www && sudo
chmod 2775 /var/www

[ec2-user@ip-10-203-10-123 ~]$ find /var/www -type d -exec sudo chmod
2775 {} + &&  find /var/www -type f -exec sudo chmod 0664 {} +

[ec2-user@ip-10-203-10-123 ~]$ mkdir /var/www/html/upload && chmod 777 /
var/www/html/upload

[ec2-user@ip-10-203-10-123 ~]$ cat <<EOF >/var/www/html/index.php
<?xml version="1.0" encoding="UTF-8" ?>
<html>
<head>
  <title>upload</title>
</head>
<body>
  <div class="upload-form">
    <h1>Upload</h1>
    <form action="upload.php" method="post" enctype="multipart/form-
data"> Your Photo:
      <input type="file" name="file" size="25" />
      <input type="submit" name="submit" value="Submit" />
    </form>
  </div>
  <div class="uploads">
    <h1>Files</h1>
    <?php
    if (\$handle = opendir('upload/')) {
      while (false !== (\$entry = readdir(\$handle))) {
        if (\$entry != "." && \$entry != "..") {
          echo "File: \$entry<br>";
        }
      }
      closedir(\$handle);
    }
    ?></div>
</body>
</html>
EOF
[ec2-user@ip-10-203-10-123 ~]$ cat <<EOF >/var/www/html/upload.php
```

```php
<?php
  move_uploaded_file(
    \$_FILES["file"]["tmp_name"],
    "upload/" . \$_FILES["file"]["name"]
  );
  header('Location: index.php');
?>
EOF
```

`[ec2-user@ip-10-203-10-123 ~]$ sudo service httpd start && sudo chkconfig httpd on`

What we have at this point is a running HTTP instance that will allow us to upload files into it. We can test that by browsing to the instance, and using the UI as shown in the following screenshot:

Next click the **Submit** button.

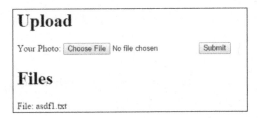

As you can see in the screenshots, we have uploaded a text document and it became available immediately. Just as we have done in the previous patterns, create an AMI from this instance using the AWS console.

It is considered best practice to remove any user or application data when creating images. In the current example, that would mean removing the file uploaded through the UI, although it is not necessary to do so to continue.

While the image is being created, we will create a load balancer for our application. Do so from the **Load Balancers** option under **NETWORK & SECURITY** in the AWS console. Follow the prompts as per your environment configuration and personal needs, making sure to add your instance in the **Add EC2 Instances** tab. Also ensure that the **Ping Path** in the **Configure Health Check** contains our index.php as seen in the following screenshot:

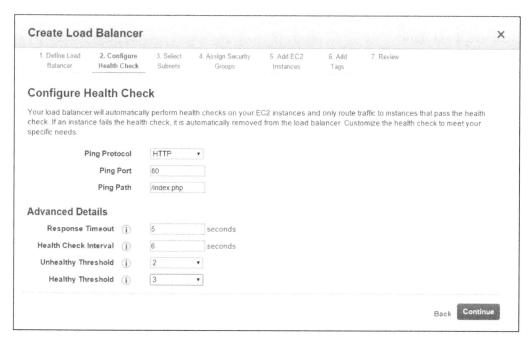

Once the image creation is complete, we will create a launch configuration for the AMI. Do so as described in the previous patterns with whatever configuration is required for your environment and personal preference but we will modify the user data heavily. For our current example, we will use rsync from the instances configured through the launch configuration in order to sync the data from the master instance to the slaves. To do this, a few things should be noted.

First, the slaves must use the proper SSH configuration to reach the master as that is the protocol that rsync uses. Next, we must ensure that a cron job exists to actually copy the data from the master to the local slave instance. Cron, without special configuration, is minute-based at the smallest iteration so that brings us to an edge case: the data will not be immediately available after being uploaded to the slaves. Lastly, we will use a virtual host proxy configuration in Apache so that the user experience does not suffer through our example.

If the user were to hit our load balancer without this configuration and refresh a few times, they might see different data each time as there is a delay between synchronization from the master to the local instance. To get around this, we will proxy their request so that the data always uploads to the master, and then synchronizes locally.

To set up this configuration, ensure that the user data, configured in the advanced portion of the **Configure details** tab for launch configuration creation, resembles the bash script as follows:

 Note that some of this will need to be modified according to your data.

```bash
#!/bin/bash
[[ ! -d /home/ec2-user/.ssh ]] && (mkdir /home/ec2-user/.ssh && chmod 644
/home/ec2-user/.ssh)
echo $'Host *\nStrictHostKeyChecking no\nHost 10.203.10.79\nIdentityFile
~/.ssh/cdr-pcs.pem' > /home/ec2-user/.ssh/config
chmod 644 /home/ec2-user/.ssh/config
cat <<EOF >/home/ec2-user/.ssh/cdr-pcs.pem
-----BEGIN RSA PRIVATE KEY-----
...your ssh key contents here....
-----END RSA PRIVATE KEY-----
EOF
chmod 400 /home/ec2-user/.ssh/cdr-pcs.pem
chown ec2-user:ec2-user /home/ec2-user -R
echo $'* * * * * ec2-user rsync -avz 10.203.10.79:/var/www/html/upload/ /
var/www/html/upload/' >> /etc/crontab
echo $'<VirtualHost *:80>\n\tServerName *\n\tProxyPass\t/
http://10.203.10.79/\n\tProxyPassReverse / http://10.203.10.79/\n</
VirtualHost>' >> /etc/httpd/conf.d/php.conf
service httpd restart
```

Once the launch configuration is completed, create an auto scaling group that references the launch configuration, and receives traffic from the load balancer that we configured as well. The remaining configuration for the auto scaling group can be decided based on your preference, but ensure that it is set to create at least one instance. When the group has been created, it will spawn a new instance into the load balancer. When all instances are shown as **InService** in the load balancer, browse to it in your web browser of choice, and upload some files. Once done, SSH into your slave instance and verify that it can, and has synced data from the master to itself.

```
marc-win8:~ $ ssh -i ~/.ssh/cdr-pcs.pem ec2-user@10.203.10.198
The authenticity of host '10.203.10.198 (10.203.10.198)' can't be
established.
ECDSA key fingerprint is 87:33:33:00:c8:ce:9b:ae:b5:22:cd:be:cb:57:cb:84.
Are you sure you want to continue connecting (yes/no)? yes
Warning: Permanently added '10.203.10.198' (ECDSA) to the list of known
hosts.
Last login: Fri Dec 19 23:11:17 2014
```

```
https://aws.amazon.com/amazon-linux-ami/2014.09-release-notes/
18 package(s) needed for security, out of 42 available
Run "sudo yum update" to apply all updates.
[ec2-user@ip-10-203-10-198 ~]$ ls /var/www/html/upload
[ec2-user@ip-10-203-10-198 ~]$ sleep 60
[ec2-user@ip-10-203-10-198 ~]$ ls /var/www/html/upload
asdf1.txt   asdf2.txt   asdf.txt
```

As we can see, through our commands we were able to upload data to the master and sync it across to our slave instance. This very crude example is a successful demonstration on how to move non-static data from instance to instance with very little frustration to the end user (hopefully).

NFS sharing pattern

While the previous example is a very crude demonstration of replicating data across thin data servers there are, no doubt, many places that could use improvement. While it did solve the problem of maintaining data across a cluster, it did not do so in real time. For the end user the problem is solved, but it does not do much to solve the overall complexity of the system.

The **Network File Sharing (NFS)** pattern aims to add real filesystem-level replication to the web application cluster by centralizing the mount point for the data. We will improve upon the original example by utilizing an underlying virtual machine whose sole purpose is to host an NFS share for the instances that are accessible through the load balancer. This provides a bit of performance increase as the underlying filesystem can be improved with little or no change to the instances that only read and write.

Again, as with all solutions, there are some benefits and concerns to be aware of. While this does simplify the access control quite a bit, it does still create a single point of failure on the NFS host itself. Unless the filesystem is replicated or clustered, if it were to experience issues, the instances accessing it would reveal the issue to the end user. To resolve this, one might abandon NFS for a distributed filesystem, such as HDFS, or GlusterFS.

 More information on GlusterFS can be found at `http://www.gluster.org/`, and information on HDFS can be found at `http://hadoop.apache.org/docs/current/hadoop-project-dist/hadoop-hdfs/HdfsUserGuide.html`.

To demonstrate this, we will first create an NFS host. Create a virtual machine, as you have done earlier, from an AWS Linux AMI, and SSH into it once it is ready:

```
[ec2-user@ip-10-203-10-161 ~]$ sudo yum install -y nfs-utils nfs-utils-lib >/dev/null 2>&1

[ec2-user@ip-10-203-10-161 ~]$ sudo mkdir /opt/shared && echo $'/opt/shared 0.0.0.0/0.0.0.0(rw,sync,no_root_squash,no_subtree_check)' | sudo tee -a /etc/exports

/opt/shared 0.0.0.0/0.0.0.0(rw)

[ec2-user@ip-10-203-10-161 ~]$ for i in rpcbind nfs nfslock; do sudo service $i start; done

Starting rpcbind:                                          [  OK  ]

Starting NFS services:                                     [  OK  ]

Starting NFS mountd:                                       [  OK  ]

Starting NFS daemon:                                       [  OK  ]

Starting RPC idmapd:                                       [  OK  ]

[ec2-user@ip-10-203-10-161 ~]$ sudo exportfs -a
```

This will create an instance that allows NFS mounting from anywhere, so be wary of your security groups and access protocols. Next, launch another instance as per your environment, based on the AWS Linux AMI. Once it is up and running, we will configure it to be an Apache HTTP server with PHP support, as well as push our base PHP files so that it becomes usable:

```
[ec2-user@ip-10-203-10-123 ~]$ sudo yum groupinstall -y "Web Server" "PHP Support" >/dev/null 2>&1

[ec2-user@ip-10-203-10-123 ~]$ sudo usermod -aG apache ec2-user

[ec2-user@ip-10-203-10-123 ~]$ sudo su ec2-user -

[ec2-user@ip-10-203-10-123 ~]$ sudo chown -R root:apache /var/www && sudo chmod 2775 /var/www
```

```
[ec2-user@ip-10-203-10-123 ~]$ find /var/www -type d -exec sudo chmod
2775 {} + &&  find /var/www -type f -exec sudo chmod 0664 {} +
[ec2-user@ip-10-203-10-123 ~]$ mkdir /var/www/html/upload
[ec2-user@ip-10-203-10-123 ~]$ echo $'10.203.10.161:/opt/shared /var/www/
html/upload nfs4 rw 0 0' | sudo tee -a /etc/fstab
[ec2-user@ip-10-203-10-123 ~]$ mount /var/www/html/upload && chmod 777 /
var/www/html/upload
[ec2-user@ip-10-203-10-123 ~]$ cat <<EOF >/var/www/html/index.php
<?xml version="1.0" encoding="UTF-8" ?>
<html>
<head>
  <title>upload</title>
</head>
<body>
  <div class="upload-form">
    <h1>Upload</h1>
    <form action="upload.php" method="post" enctype="multipart/form-
data"> Your Photo:
      <input type="file" name="file" size="25" />
      <input type="submit" name="submit" value="Submit" />
    </form>
  </div>
  <div class="uploads">
    <h1>Files</h1>
    <?php
    if (\$handle = opendir('upload/')) {
      while (false !== (\$entry = readdir(\$handle))) {
        if (\$entry != "." && \$entry != "..") {
          echo "File: \$entry<br>";
        }
      }
      closedir(\$handle);
    }
    ?></div>
</body>
</html>
EOF
```

```
[ec2-user@ip-10-203-10-123 ~]$ cat <<EOF >/var/www/html/upload.php
<?php
  move_uploaded_file(
    \$_FILES["file"]["tmp_name"],
    "upload/" . \$_FILES["file"]["name"]
  );
  header('Location: index.php');
?>
EOF
[ec2-user@ip-10-203-10-123 ~]$ sudo service httpd start
```

What we have at this point is a running HTTP instance that will allow us to upload files into it. We can test that by browsing to the instance and using the UI as seen in the following:

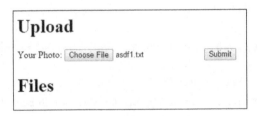

Next, click **Submit**.

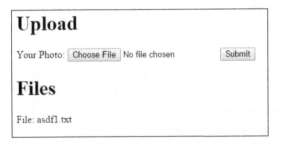

As you can see in the preceding screenshots, we have uploaded a text document and it became available immediately. Just as we have done in the previous patterns, create an AMI from this instance using the AWS console.

While the image is being created, we will create a load balancer for our application. Do so from the **Load Balancers** option under **NETWORK & SECURITY** in the AWS console. Follow the prompts as per your environment configuration and personal needs, making sure to add your instance at the **Add EC2 Instances** tab. Also ensure that the **Ping Path** in the **Configure Health Check** contains our `index.php`, as seen in the following screenshot:

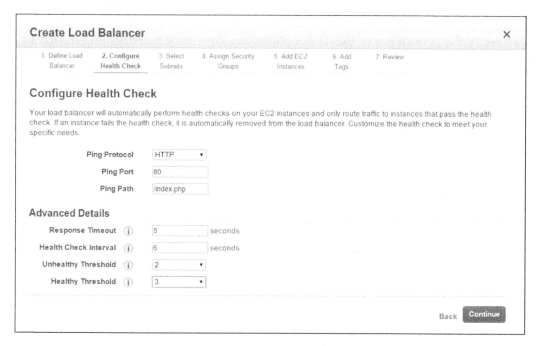

Once the image creation is complete, we will create a launch configuration for the AMI. Do so as described in the previous patterns with whatever configuration that is required for your environment and personal preference, but we will modify the user data slightly. To set up this configuration, ensure that the user data configured in the advanced portion of the **Configure details** tab for launch configuration creation, resembles the bash as follows:

```
#!/bin/bash
chmod 777 /var/www/html/upload
service httpd start
```

A very noticeable difference between this pattern and the previous one is the large truncation of the user data. Once the launch configuration is completed, create an auto scaling group that references the launch configuration, and receives traffic from the load balancer that we configured. The remaining configuration for the auto scaling group can be decided based on your preference, but ensure it is set to create at least one instance. When the group has been created, it will spawn a new instance into the load balancer. When all instances are shown as **InService** in the load balancer, browse to it in your web browser of choice, and upload some files. We can verify the persistence of the data replication more easily by refreshing the load balancer in our web browser and uploading multiple files. Each time you upload and refresh the page, the data stays persistent with no proxying required.

State sharing pattern

The previous patterns have aimed at dynamic content handling in the form of uploaded content. But it is obvious to most system administrators that this is not the only form of dynamic content in a system. Besides being able to upload and download files themselves, dynamic data can exist in the form of session data or state information. Imagine for a moment, a very simple server setup that consists of a web application in the form of a user management page and a database.

One system might compose the database while the other system handles the user management of the application. To do this, a user must log in with credentials to manipulate the data that comes in and out of the database server. If the system has no other components then when the user logs in, this information is retained in memory. This is not a good practice as memory itself is volatile and restricted in size. If a lot of users were to log in, or the system had to be rebooted, then the user would have to log in again.

In a more complex setup, we might put the web application behind a load balancer, which poses an immediate problem to the current setup: the information stored in memory. This is resolved with key value stores, such as Redis, MemCached, or the AWS-provided ElastiCache service. While Redis and MemCached are extremely good at this, we will use ElastiCache for this example as it is provided by AWS, is the best among these services, and requires very little from an operational standpoint. We will create a small scalable login system that uses this server, to demonstrate the power of a **Key Value Store (KVS)**.

 More information on Redis can be found at http://redis.io, while information on MemCached can be found at http://memcached.org/.

First, browse to the **ElastiCache** section of the AWS console. Once there, select **Redis** as the engine, as it is my personal preference, and select **Next**.

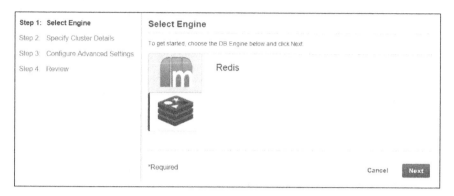

On the **Specify Cluster Details** screen, you may leave all defaults, or modify according to your environment. Be sure to add the required fields, such as **Replication Group Name** and **Replication Group Description**; select **Next**.

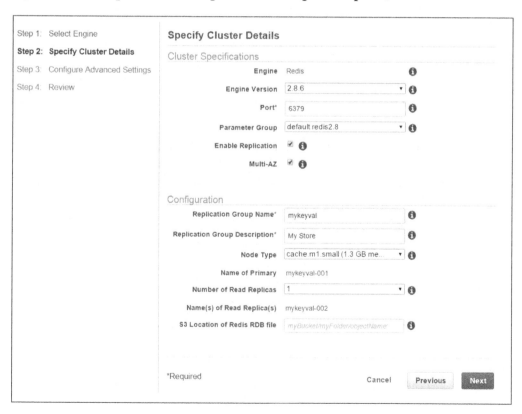

At the **Configure Advanced Settings** tab, you may leave all defaults or modify as per your environment. Now select **Next,** and then the **Launch Replication Group**.

Step 1: Select Engine	**Configure Advanced Settings**
Step 2: Specify Cluster Details	Network & Security
Step 3: Configure Advanced Settings	Cache Subnet Group: cache (vpc-) ▾ ❶
Step 4: Review	Availability Zone(s) ❶

Network & Security

Cache Subnet Group   cache (vpc-   )   ▾ ❶

Availability Zone(s)   ❶

Primary   mykeyval-001   us-east-1a ▾

Read Replica(s)   mykeyval-002   us-east-1c ▾

VPC Security Group(s)
- launch-wizard-1 (vpc-   ...
- local (vpc-   )
- pilot-vcp-access (vpc-   ...
- nat-internal (vpc-   )   ❶

Backup

Enable Automatic Backups   ☐ ❶

Maintenance

Maintenance Window   ○ Select Window ◉ No Preference ❶

Topic for SNS Notification*   Disable Notifications ▾   Manual ARN input ❶

*Required   Cancel   Previous   **Next**

This will create a KVS store that is usable once the creation is complete. Next, let's demonstrate how to interact with Redis. In the following code, we will use the rubygem `redis` to connect to the `Redis` server, check its status, input a key/value pair, and finally retrieve the value:

```
marc-win8:~ $ gem install redis
Fetching: redis-3.2.0.gem (100%)
Successfully installed redis-3.2.0
Parsing documentation for redis-3.2.0
Installing ri documentation for redis-3.2.0
Done installing documentation for redis after 2 seconds
1 gem installed
marc-win8:~ $ irb
irb(main):001:0> require 'redis'
=> true
```

```
irb(main):002:0> r = Redis.new(:host => "10.203.10.160", :port => 6380,
:db => 15)
=> #<Redis client v3.2.0 connected to redis://10.203.10.160:6380/0 (Redis
v2.8.6)>
irb(main):003:0> r.ping
=> "PONG"
irb(main):004:0> r.set('foo','bar')
=> "OK"
irb(main):005:0> r.get('foo')
=> "bar"
```

What we have done at this point is created a permanent key foo with the value bar. Since it is from an AWS-provided KVS, we know that the data is persistent and resilient. Because the data is permanent, we can swap the front-end instances ad-hoc and know that any data stored into it will not change. What we would do now from a development standpoint is use this key value store on authentication to store the session or cookie information that is unique to the user.

From pages that require authorization, we would use their cookie information provided in the HTTP headers to authorize the action into the page. The benefit to a state store, such as Redis, or MemCached, is that any key can have a **Time To Live** (**TTL**) set on it during initialization. This means that if the request is made after the TTL has expired, the value fails the look-up. An example of this would be to set a one-day TTL when a user logs in so that they must log in daily.

 More information on the Redis ruby client can be found at their GitHub page at https://github.com/redis/redis-rb.

URL rewriting pattern

In the spirit of utilizing previous patterns, as well as AWS-provided services, we might combine the previous examples, which allow uploading files into an instance, with S3 instead of using a shared filesystem such as NFS. One problem with the previous examples is that there exists a single point of failure.

In the clone server pattern, the slaves synchronize files from a non-redundant master instance. In the NFS sharing pattern, all of the instances use a filesystem provided by an instance that is non-redundant as well. From an operations standpoint this adds some theoretical failure points. Instead of pushing the files into these instances, we could use something like S3.

We would do this by rewriting requests for files on-the-fly using Apache's filter module or Nginx's proxy rewrite functionality. For this example, we will assume an Nginx configuration instead of Apache for ease of demonstration.

The PHP files in this chapter will look similar to those in the previous chapter. In fact index.php will require no changes. The file upload.php, however, will require some modification. Instead of writing to the local filesystem (or NFS as displayed in the previous example), we would write to an S3 bucket. First ensure the S3 bucket is unique, serves HTML as a static web server as demonstrated in the examples in *Chapter 2, Basic Patterns*, and contains a sub-directory upload.

Next, modify the upload.php file to upload to S3 instead of writing into the local filesystem. The code for that might look similar to the following:

```php
<?php
use Aws\S3\S3Client;

$bucket = '*** Your Bucket Name ***';
$keyname = '*** Your Object Key ***';
$filepath = '/tmp/' . uniqid();
move_uploaded_file(
  $_FILES["file"]["tmp_name"],
  $filepath
);

$s3 = S3Client::factory();

$result = $s3->putObject(array(
    'Bucket'      => $bucket,
    'Key'         => $keyname,
    'SourceFile'  => $filepath
));
header('Location: index.php');
?>
```

This will successfully upload the file from a temporary location on the local system into S3. To actually utilize this, we must rewrite incoming requests with a 301 redirect into the S3 instance. If we assume that the only thing that the user has to upload is image data in JPEG format, we would put this into our Nginx configuration file:

```
location ~ img\/.+\.jpg\$ {
   return 301 http://31d1f38f-fc88-4899-a382-7a42e9444ec5.s3-website-
us-east-1.amazonaws.com\$uri;
}
```

Any HTML that links to an image, such as:

```
<img src="upload/image.jpg"/>
```

will receive a redirect, and retrieve the object from S3, via HTTP. This allows us to use S3 as an object store for dynamic data, and builds in a new layer of redundancy and resiliency to our application. With these tweaks, we no longer need a running master instance, or a running filesystem instance so we can spin up new worker instances ad-hoc.

Cache proxy pattern

Let's step back to the original issue of managing a web application that contains dynamic data. We have covered a few different patterns in this chapter that optimize the redundancy at the file level, from distributed filesystems, to master-slave replication, and finally through the S3 offload of uploaded data.

While all of these aim to solve the problem from an operational perspective, we have not touched heavily on optimization to the end user, which is arguably the most important factor. Some patterns introduce delay in retrieval, and discrepancies in the form of data not persisting through subsequent HTTP requests. The best optimization to the end user, and the easiest to demonstrate, is retrieval optimization. This could be done through a CDN as we have discussed earlier in some static data processing patterns, but that does not work well with dynamic data.

The problem with dynamic data and a CDN is delay through replication. CloudFront takes an arguably long amount of time to replicate outwards so that does not solve the delay issue for the user. The easiest way to solve this is through caching the objects themselves. There are quite a few different pieces of software that mitigate this, such as Varnish and Squid. I will demonstrate a simple Varnish cache server along with our tried-and-true PHP uploader.

 More information on Varnish can be found at `https://www.varnish-cache.org/`, and that on Squid can be found at `http://www.squid-cache.org/`.

The first instance will be our HTTP server, so let's spin up an EC2 instance based on the AWS Linux AMI as we have done earlier. Once it is up and running, we will SSH into it, and configure it as we have done before:

```
[ec2-user@ip-10-203-10-200 ~]$ sudo yum groupinstall -y "Web Server" "PHP Support" >/dev/null 2>&1
[ec2-user@ip-10-203-10-200 ~]$ sudo usermod -aG apache ec2-user
```

```
[ec2-user@ip-10-203-10-200 ~]$ sudo su ec2-user -

[ec2-user@ip-10-203-10-200 ~]$ sudo chown -R root:apache /var/www && sudo
chmod 2775 /var/www

[ec2-user@ip-10-203-10-200 ~]$ find /var/www -type d -exec sudo chmod
2775 {} + &&  find /var/www -type f -exec sudo chmod 0664 {} +

[ec2-user@ip-10-203-10-200 ~]$ mkdir /var/www/html/upload && chmod 777 /
var/www/html/upload

[ec2-user@ip-10-203-10-200 ~]$ cat <<EOF >/var/www/html/index.php

<?xml version="1.0" encoding="UTF-8" ?>

<html>

<head>

  <title>upload</title>

</head>

<body>

  <div class="upload-form">

    <h1>Upload</h1>

    <form action="upload.php" method="post" enctype="multipart/form-
data"> Your Photo:

      <input type="file" name="file" size="25" />

      <input type="submit" name="submit" value="Submit" />

    </form>

  </div>

  <div class="uploads">

    <h1>Files</h1>

    <?php

      if (\$handle = opendir('upload/')) {

        while (false !== (\$entry = readdir(\$handle))) {

          if (\$entry != "." && \$entry != "..") {

            echo "File: \$entry<br>";

          }

        }

        closedir(\$handle);

      }

    ?></div>

</body>

</html>

EOF
```

```
[ec2-user@ip-10-203-10-200 ~]$ cat <<EOF >/var/www/html/upload.php
<?php
  move_uploaded_file(
    \$_FILES["file"]["tmp_name"],
    "upload/" . \$_FILES["file"]["name"]
  );
  header('Location: index.php');
?>
EOF
[ec2-user@ip-10-203-10-200 ~]$ sudo service httpd start
```

Now that the instance is running, we will create a Varnish server that points to this single instance. Launch another EC2 instance based on the AWS Linux AMI, and SSH into it once it is available.

 Note that some of the following lines may require adjusting as per your environment specifications.

```
[ec2-user@ip-10-203-10-187 ~]$ sudo yum install -y http://yum.puppetlabs.
com/puppetlabs-release-el-6.noarch.rpm >/dev/null 2>&1
[ec2-user@ip-10-203-10-187 ~]$ sudo yum install -y puppet >/dev/null 2>&1
[ec2-user@ip-10-203-10-187 ~]$ sudo mkdir /etc/puppet/modules
[ec2-user@ip-10-203-10-187 ~]$ sudo puppet module install maxchk-varnish
dnsdomainname: Unknown host
Preparing to install into /etc/puppet/modules ...
Downloading from http://forge.puppetlabs.com ...
Installing -- do not interrupt ...
/etc/puppet/modules
└── maxchk-varnish (v0.0.6)


[ec2-user@ip-10-203-10-187 ~]$ cat <<EOF >/tmp/setup.pp
class {'varnish':
  varnish_listen_port => 80,
  varnish_storage_size => '1G',
}
class { 'varnish::vcl':
  probes => [
```

```
      { name => 'health_check', url => "/index.php" },
  ],
  backends => [
      { name => 'server1', host => '10.203.10.220', port => '80', probe =>
'health_check' },
  ],
  directors => [
      { name => 'cluster', type => 'round-robin', backends => [ 'server1' ]
}
  ],
  selectors => [
      { backend => 'cluster' },
  ],
}
EOF
[ec2-user@ip-10-203-10-187 ~]$ sudo puppet apply /tmp/setup.pp

dnsdomainname: Unknown host

dnsdomainname: Unknown host

notice: /Stage[main]/Varnish::Install/Package[varnish]/ensure: created

notice: /Stage[main]/Varnish::Vcl/File[varnish-vcl]/content: content
changed '{md5}3c5af7ddff1cfe34b5f6ea7e321c0145' to '{md5}57316613af12efec
cb32f27b64d51900'

notice: /Stage[main]/Varnish::Shmlog/Mount[shmlog-mount]/ensure: defined
'ensure' as 'mounted'

notice: /Stage[main]/Varnish::Shmlog/Mount[shmlog-mount]: Triggered
'refresh' from 1 events

notice: /Stage[main]/Varnish/File[varnish-conf]/ensure: created

notice: /Stage[main]/Varnish::Service/Service[varnish]/ensure: ensure
changed 'stopped' to 'running'

notice: /Stage[main]/Varnish::Service/Service[varnish]: Triggered
'refresh' from 2 events

notice: /Stage[main]/Varnish/File[storage-dir]/ensure: created

notice: Finished catalog run in 7.06 seconds
```

We now have a running Varnish server that listens to port 6081, and forwards requests to a cluster of one, or the instance that we created earlier. If you browse to port 6081 on this instance, you will see the File upload HTTP page as always. You may upload files at will, but you would notice that subsequent visits and refreshes stay relatively small in size. As the page grows with uploads, the process will stay consistent.

It is obvious with this example, as with the others, that there is still room for improvement. As this example currently stands, we cannot cluster it traditionally as we have the others, since the load balancer does not know of the lower application instances, but only of the Varnish server. To solve this problem, we would choose a service discovery module, such as Consul, instead of using auto scaling Groups and launch configurations.

 Information on Consul service discovery and Varnish can be seen at the Hashicorp blog at `https://hashicorp.com/blog/introducing-consul-template.html`.

Another point to be made is that we have introduced the original issue of the files not being replicated across servers. If we were to combine this pattern with Consul service discovery and the steps taken in the previous pattern to store the files within S3, we would have a complete web application tier. This complete tier still contains a single point of failure, however, on the Varnish server itself.

If we wished to use turtles all the way down, so-to-speak, we could use S3 or a distributed filesystem, such as `GlusterFS` for the cache data on the Varnish server. Through this we could add as many Varnish servers as needed, and make them accessible through the load balancer, at which point our application would have proper caching, load balancing, fail over, cache, and data redundancy and replication. The system administrator within us most likely favors this tier.

Summary

In this chapter, we covered quite a few patterns to discuss how to handle data that is dynamic. In the clone server pattern, we demonstrated how to maintain data on a master instance, and clone it to slave instances. This allowed us to scale out and not miss any data. Next we moved to the NFS sharing pattern in which we used a single data store under NFS to hold the data. This allowed us to scale out without having any point-in-time issues with our data. We then moved to the state sharing pattern where we demonstrated the use of a key-value store, such as ElastiCache, and touched on some examples of how to add this into our infrastructure. We then moved to the URL rewriting pattern in which we demonstrated how we could move all of our static assets, such as images and JavaScript files, into S3 and rewrite them from the HTTP server, without any user disruption. Lastly we talked on the cache proxy pattern in which we optimized the user experience further by caching the static assets from the previous example.

Next we will move on to patterns for uploading data.

6

Patterns for Uploading Data

Most system administrators and developers are very familiar with data being uploaded to servers. From HTTP servers (with upload forms) to FTP servers, it is common to come across variations in how to handle the upload as well as the data. For developers, the issue is where to store the data and how to access the interface. Common examples would be using REST to proxy the file to another system or perhaps just writing it into the file system.

From the system administrators' perspective, the questions go a little deeper. If the files will be stored on the filesystem, how will it be able to scale across multiple instances? If it is going to interact with another system, are the system administrators responsible for that instance as well? Were any dependencies introduced, such as database tables or rows? These questions almost come back full-circle to previous patterns and issues such as high availability and redundancy.

We have previously touched upon simple file uploads in patterns such as the clone server pattern, where we added redundancy through a simple master/slave setup, and the NFS sharing pattern, where we used a shared filesystem to avoid duplicating data and issues of master failover.

In this chapter, we will be a bit more creative in terms of how to overall handle the uploads instead of only looking at them from a data redundancy point of view. We will do this by utilizing S3 storage as much as possible for the data as that will remove the need for data replication and failover altogether, albeit with some side effects.

Uploading data through HTML forms into the filesystem is native to most HTTP servers. However, uploading it into something such as S3, is not. Because of this, we will introduce a few methods of interacting with S3. You will see how we handle this barrier using the patterns discussed in the following sections.

In this chapter, we will cover the following patterns:

- Write proxy pattern
- Storage index pattern
- Direct object upload pattern

Write proxy pattern

The first method we will discuss for handling uploaded data will be quite different than any method thus far. Instead of uploading through the HTTP front-end as before, we will handle the data through a different protocol. It is not often to see a web server as the only means for sending data into a server. Legacy systems, systems that wish to support extremely large files, or even systems that need the transfer to be as optimized as possible would typically not interact via the HTML POST method.

Some examples of protocols used for file uploads that one might typically find, are:

- FTP or SFTP
- FTPS or SCP
- HTTP PUT/POST
- UDP optimized transfers such as Tsunami UDP

 More information on Tsunami can be found at `http://tsunami-udp.sourceforge.net/`.

For this example, we will use FTP as it is a bit easy to demonstrate and requires little overhead. This pattern allows the end user to anonymously upload the data via FTP into a proxy server, whose only purpose is to move the uploaded data into S3.

This pattern helps to relieve some side effects from other patterns in which data was uploaded. The previous patterns, clone server pattern and NFS sharing pattern, allowed uploads via HTTP POST but had to resolve data synchronization between machines at scale time as well as redundancy of the data itself. However, if we use the Amazon-provided S3 service, we get synchronization support and data redundancy out of the box. This resolves the issue of what happens to the data if any (or all) of the instances go down.

Another huge benefit to this pattern, which isn't covered in the example, is that it can be scaled horizontally with very little additional effort. If the FTP server is cloned and all of these instances are put behind a load balancer, we could upload to whichever instance was chosen for us to connect to. Since the data is offloaded into S3, and the web server only cares about what is in the S3 bucket, there is no side effect to either set of the end users: those using the web server and those uploading data. The web server could also be cloned and scaled horizontally, since it is using the S3 API to retrieve and list the objects.

The machine will provide anonymous FTP access with write access to the end user. Once data is uploaded, the server will synchronize that data to an S3 bucket with HTTP serving enabled. It will service a web page as it did before but will not allow uploads through it as we have. Instead, it will simply list the files available within the S3 bucket and allow the end user to download them through the web server interface.

As with all of our patterns, it is not perfect out of the box by any means and introduces side effects relative to the problem it is solving. We will not be configuring the FTP server process to run a command when uploads finish. While it is possible, it takes quite a bit of added configuration for a multitude of reasons (the biggest being that the official ProFTPd module to do this does not support chroot with anonymous access). Instead, we will be using a third-party package, incrond, which monitors a directory for changes and runs commands on a notify signal.

This example uses AWS Linux, and while at one point in time this Linux distribution was very closely mirrored to the CentOS distribution, it has strayed very far away in recent developments. We will be installing a package built specifically for RedHat architecture EL6, which is never recommended for the AWS Linux distribution.

Another note to be made about this example is that it can be divided into two separate systems: one for the web server and one for the FTP server. Next, please note that as mentioned before, uploads into S3 are not immediately available. Lastly, if the FTP server for this pattern was scaled horizontally, as described earlier, the only issue might be data integrity. If multiple users attempted to upload files with the same filenames in the same location, it would be a race condition for which version made it into S3. This could be resolved, however, by giving unique filenames and data locations to each user.

Let's get started by first creating an S3 bucket. Do as we did before, making sure to enable website hosting with a bucket policy that allows objects to be retrieved. Once that is done, launch an instance based on the AWS Linux AMI as per your environment. Once it is ready, SSH into it and configure it to be an FTP server:

```
[ec2-user]$ sudo yum install -y gcc gcc-c++ >/dev/null 2>&1
[ec2-user]$ curl -s ftp://ftp.proftpd.org/distrib/source/proftpd-
1.3.5.tar.gz > proftpd-1.3.5.tar.gz
[ec2-user]$ tar zxf proftpd-1.3.5.tar.gz
[ec2-user]$ cd proftpd-1.3.5
[ec2-user]$ ./configure -sysconfdir=/etc --with-modules=mod_exec >/dev/
null 2>&1
[ec2-user]$ make >/dev/null 2>&1
[ec2-user]$ sudo make install >/dev/null 2>&1
[ec2-user]$ sudo ln -s /usr/local/sbin/proftpd /usr/sbin/proftpd
[ec2-user]$ sudo cp contrib/dist/rpm/proftpd.init.d /etc/init.d/proftpd
[ec2-user]$ sudo chmod +x /etc/init.d/proftpd
[ec2-user]$ sudo cp sample-configurations/anonymous.conf /etc/proftpd.
conf
[ec2-user]$ sudo sed -i.bak 's/nobody\|nogroup/ftp/g' /etc/proftpd.conf
[ec2-user]$ cd ~
[ec2-user]$ export IP=$(curl -s http://169.254.169.254/latest/meta-data/
local-ipv4)
[ec2-user]$ sudo mkdir /var/log/proftpd && sudo chmod 744 /var/log/
proftpd && sudo chown ftp:ftp /var/log/proftpd
[ec2-user]$ echo "DefaultAddress  ${IP}"$'\nSocketBindTight\ton\
nServerLog /var/log/proftpd/server.log\nTransferLog /var/log/proftpd/
xfer.log' | sudo tee -a /etc/proftpd.conf >/dev/null
[ec2-user]$ sudo mkdir -p /var/ftp/uploads && sudo chown ftp:ftp /var/ftp
-R && sudo chmod 777 /var/ftp -R
[ec2-user]$ sudo service proftpd start
Starting proftpd:                                           [  OK  ]
[ec2-user]$ sudo yum install -y http://pkgs.repoforge.org/incron/
incron-0.5.9-2.el6.rf.x86_64.rpm >/dev/null 2>&1
[ec2-user]$ echo $'#!/bin/sh\nexport AWS_ACCESS_KEY_ID=myaccesskey\
nexport AWS_SECRET_ACCESS_KEY=mysecretkey\nexport AWS_DEFAULT_REGION=us-
east-1' | sudo tee -a /etc/profile.d/aws.sh >/dev/null
[ec2-user]$ sudo chmod +x /etc/profile.d/aws.sh
[ec2-user]$ sudo touch /usr/local/bin/ftp2s3.sh && sudo chown ftp:ftp /
usr/local/bin/ftp2s3.sh && sudo chmod +x /usr/local/bin/ftp2s3.sh
[ec2-user]$ cat <<EOF | sudo tee -a /usr/local/bin/ftp2s3.sh >/dev/null
> #!/bin/bash
> . /etc/profile.d/aws.sh
```

```
> cd /var/ftp/uploads
> aws s3 sync s3://31d1f38f-fc88-4899-a382-7a42e9444ec5 . >>/var/log/
proftpd/sync.log 2>&1
> aws s3 sync . s3://31d1f38f-fc88-4899-a382-7a42e9444ec5 >>/var/log/
proftpd/sync.log 2>&1
> EOF
[ec2-user]$ echo ftp | sudo tee -a /etc/incron.allow >/dev/null
[ec2-user]$ echo root | sudo tee -a /etc/incron.allow >/dev/null
[ec2-user]$ echo /var/ftp/uploads IN_CREATE /usr/local/bin/ftp2s3.sh |
sudo tee -a /etc/incron.d/proftpd
[ec2-user]$ sudo service incrond start
Starting Filesystem event daemon (incrond):      [ OK ]
```

We can go ahead at this point and upload a file to it via SFTP, and verify that it appears in our S3 bucket:

```
C:\Users\marcus.young\book
$ aws s3 ls s3://31d1f38f-fc88-4899-a382-7a42e9444ec5


C:\Users\marcus.young\book
$ ftp 10.203.10.52
Connected to 10.203.10.52.
220 ProFTPD 1.3.5 Server (ProFTPD Anonymous Server) [10.203.10.52]
User (10.203.10.52:(none)): anonymous
331 Anonymous login ok, send your complete email address as your password
Password:
230 Anonymous access granted, restrictions apply
ftp> CD uploads
250 CWD command successful
ftp> PUT file1
200 PORT command successful
150 Opening ASCII mode data connection for file1
226 Transfer complete
ftp: 7 bytes sent in 0.31Seconds 0.02Kbytes/sec.
ftp> PUT file2
200 PORT command successful
150 Opening ASCII mode data connection for file2
226 Transfer complete
ftp: 7 bytes sent in 0.21Seconds 0.03Kbytes/sec.
ftp> quit
221 Goodbye.
```

```
C:\Users\marcus.young\Downloads\book
$ aws s3 ls s3://31d1f38f-fc88-4899-a382-7a42e9444ec5
2014-12-31 11:28:59        6 file1
2014-12-31 11:28:59        6 file2
```

At this point, we have a working proxy server. However, we will take it a step further and add an HTTP front-end to list and retrieve the files from S3. You may either spin up a new instance identical to the last or use the existing instance. Whichever choice is made, SSH into it when it is ready:

```
[ec2-user]$ sudo yum groupinstall -y "Web Server" "PHP Support" >/dev/
null 2>&1
[ec2-user]$ sudo usermod -aG apache ec2-user
[ec2-user]$ sudo su ec2-user -
[ec2-user]$ sudo chown -R root:apache /var/www && sudo chmod 2775 /var/
www
[ec2-user]$ find /var/www -type d -exec sudo chmod 2775 {} + &&  find /
var/www -type f -exec sudo chmod 0664 {} +
[ec2-user]$ mkdir /var/www/html/upload && chmod 777 /var/www/html/upload
[ec2-user]$ cd /var/www/html
[ec2-user]$ (
>    curl -sS https://getcomposer.org/installer | php
>    echo '{"require": {"aws/aws-sdk-php": "2.6.*"}}' >composer.json
>    php composer.phar install
> ) >/dev/null 2>&1
[ec2-user]$ echo $'#!/bin/sh\nexport AWS_ACCESS_KEY_ID=myaccesskey\
nexport AWS_SECRET_ACCESS_KEY=mysecretkey' | sudo tee -a /etc/sysconfig/
httpd >/dev/null
[ec2-user]$ cat <<EOF >/var/www/html/index.php
> <?php
>    require 'vendor/autoload.php';
>
>    use Aws\S3\S3Client;
>    use Aws\S3\Exception\S3Exception;
>
>    \$bucket = '31d1f38f-fc88-4899-a382-7a42e9444ec5';
>
>    \$client = S3Client::factory(array(
>        'key'    => \$_ENV["AWS_ACCESS_KEY_ID"],
>        'secret' => \$_ENV["AWS_SECRET_ACCESS_KEY"],
>    ));
> ?>
> <?xml version="1.0" encoding="UTF-8" ?>
```

```
>  <html>
>  <head>
>    <title>upload</title>
>  </head>
>  <body>
>    <div class="upload-form">
>       <h1>Upload</h1>
>       <div class="uploads">
>       <h1>Files</h1>
>          <?php
>             \$objects = \$client->getIterator('ListObjects', array('Bucket'
=> \$bucket));
>
>          foreach (\$objects as \$object) {
>                echo "<a href=\"http://" . \$bucket . ".s3-website-us-
east-1.amazonaws.com/" . \$object['Key'] . "\">" . \$object['Key'] . "</
a><br/>";
>          }
>          ?>
>
>    </div>
>  </body>
>  </html>
>  EOF
[ec2-user]$ sudo service httpd start
Starting httpd: httpd: apr_sockaddr_info_get() failed for ip-10-203-10-52
httpd: Could not reliably determine the server's fully qualified domain
name, using 127.0.0.1 for ServerName
                                         [  OK  ]
```

The previous snippet will set up our Apache HTTP server and configure PHP as well
as the AWS API. If we browse to our instance via a web browser, we will be greeted
by a handy list of files that can be retrieved from S3 as a link.

Files

file1
file2

Storage index pattern

If you are following along with the patterns, you might notice that the previous pattern is a bit slow to display from the web server. When we iterated over the objects through the PHP API, there were a lot of calls being made in the background, such as SSL handshakes, IAM authorization for the calls and objects themselves, and so on.

We could improve heavily on the previous example by indexing the files that are to be uploaded. The proxy server that uploads to S3 could cache or store metadata about the file. This would ensure that the user gets a much quicker response, instead of waiting for the S3 calls to complete on each refresh of the web server. It should also be noted that without this improvement, the number of API calls is directly proportional to the number of end users hitting the web server. Amazon's S3 billing model is by API usage, so the cost goes up as the number of users and the amount of usage goes up. Management might be silently thankful for a heavily loaded system that includes caching.

The way we will improve on the previous system is by creating a database that stores the information about the file just after it has been written to the S3 bucket. First, we will launch an RDS instance. Configure it as per your environment by clicking **Launch DB Instance** from **RDS Dashboard**.

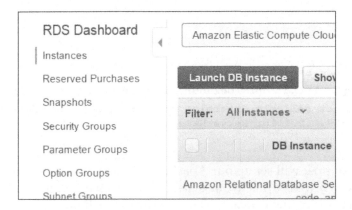

From the **Select Engine** tab, use the default of MySQL and click **Select**. Select whatever is appropriate for you in the **Production?** tab and click **Next Step**. Make note of your administration information such as username and password from the **Specify DB Details** tab and click **Next Step**. Finish relevant configuration in the **Configure Advanced Settings** tab, and then select **Launch DB Instance** to complete. View your instance by selecting **View Your DB Instances** from the final confirmation window. Make note of the hostname, named **Endpoint**, for your instance by selecting it in the **Instances** tab of the RDS console.

If the instance or instances from the previous pattern are still running, we will continue to use them. Otherwise, if you wish to follow along, follow the process from the previous example to configure a running virtual machine with an FTP server and a web server. Once it is configured and running, we will gather our first metric to base our optimization goal upon:

```
$ time curl -s http://10.203.10.159 >/dev/null
```

```
real    0m6.086s
user    0m0.015s
sys     0m0.000s
```

The previous command shows that a curl to our web server took just over six seconds to complete using the S3 API! From an end user's perspective, this is most likely unacceptable. From our running instance, let's first configure MySQL with a database and a very simple table for metadata storage:

```
[ec2-user@ip-10-203-10-159 ~]$ sudo yum install -y mysql >/dev/null
[ec2-user@ip-10-203-10-159 ~]$ sudo yum install php-mysql
[ec2-user@ip-10-203-10-159 ~]$ cat <<EOF | mysql -umydbuser -pabc1234\!
-hmydbinstance.cndulnje6en1.us-east-1.rds.amazonaws.com
> create database mys3info;
> use mys3info;create table files (
> id INT AUTO_INCREMENT PRIMARY KEY,
> filename varchar(50),
> location varchar(50)
> );
> EOF
```

In our previous example, we created a script that is run each time a file changes on the proxy server from FTP uploads. We will reconfigure that script to insert metadata into the MySQL table after the S3 synchronization completes:

```
[ec2-user@ip-10-203-10-159 ~]$ cat <<EOF >/usr/local/bin/ftp2s3.sh
> #!/bin/bash
> . /etc/profile.d/aws.sh
> upload_location="/var/ftp/uploads"
> cd ${upload_location}
> aws s3 sync s3://31d1f38f-fc88-4899-a382-7a42e9444ec5 . >>/var/log/
proftpd/sync.log 2>&1
>
> IFS='\n'; for i in `aws s3 sync . s3://31d1f38f-fc88-4899-a382-
7a42e9444ec5`; do
>    #the output gets really dirty here. For the sake of a demo...
>    clean=$(echo $i | sed 's/^.\+upload:/upload:/g' | awk '{print $2}' |
grep -E '^\.')
>    if [[ -n $clean ]]; then
>      filename=$(basename $clean)
>      cat <<EOF | mysql -umydbuser -pabc1234\! -hmydbinstance.
cndulnje6en1.us-east-1.rds.amazonaws.com mys3info
>      insert into files(filename, location) values('${filename}',
'${upload_location}');
> EOF
>    fi
> done
```

This script, which should absolutely not be used in a real production system ever, will insert the filename of the item or items uploaded into the MySQL table. We can check that by uploading a file via FTP and viewing the rows from the table:

```
[ec2-user@ip-10-203-10-159 ~]$ mysql -umydbuser -pabc1234\!
-hmydbinstance.cndulnje6en1.us-east-1.rds.amazonaws.com mys3info -e
'select * from files;'
+----+----------+------------------+
| id | filename | location         |
+----+----------+------------------+
| 1  | file3    | /var/ftp/uploads |
| 2  | file2    | /var/ftp/uploads |
+----+----------+------------------+
```

For the end user, however, the problem is not solved. When the web page is requested, the S3 API is still used. Instead, we will use a database query. Let's modify the PHP page:

```
[ec2-user@ip-10-203-10-159 ~]$ cat <<EOF >/var/www/html/index.php
> <?php
>    \$bucket = '31d1f38f-fc88-4899-a382-7a42e9444ec5';
>    \$conn = mysql_connect('mydbinstance.cndulnje6en1.us-east-1.rds.
amazonaws.com', 'mydbuser', 'abc1234!');
>    \$db = mysql_select_db('mys3info');
>
> ?>
> <?xml version="1.0" encoding="UTF-8" ?>
> <html>
> <head>
>    <title>upload</title>
> </head>
> <body>
>    <div class="uploads">
>       <h1>Files</h1>
>       <?php
>
>          \$sql = "SELECT filename FROM files";
>          \$result = mysql_query(\$sql);
>
>          while (\$row = mysql_fetch_assoc(\$result)) {
>             echo "<a href=\"http://" . \$bucket . ".s3-website-us-east-1.
amazonaws.com/" . \$row['filename'] . "\">" . \$row['filename'] . "</
a><br/>";
>          }
>       ?>
>
>    </div>
> </body>
> </html>
> EOF
```

We can verify that it works as expected by browsing to our instance via a web browser.

Lastly, we should verify that this is a much quicker response to the end user:

```
$ time curl -s http://10.203.10.159 >/dev/null

real    0m0.425s
user    0m0.000s
sys     0m0.030s
```

Direct object upload pattern

In this last pattern, we will try to resolve the original issue in a different way rather than optimize on the original attempt. The problem we are facing is how to handle data that needs to be uploaded to a central store. We would like to stay with Amazon-provided services as much as possible, so what we will attempt to do here is demonstrate direct upload into S3 from a web server.

In both the write proxy pattern and the storage index pattern, we allowed the user to upload into S3 using an FTP server as a proxy. S3 itself has a very robust HTTP POST support and allows S3 access via HTTP methods, even without being configured for static website access, as we currently have enabled on our bucket.

For this pattern, we will set up a web instance with only the Apache HTTP web server on it, which contains a form to upload into our bucket. For the form to POST successfully, however, some steps must be taken to allow proper authorization from our server itself. We will create a ruby script that creates the proper authorization pieces our form needs, and configure the HTML form to use these values.

Launch an instance from the AWS Linux AMI and SSH into it when it is ready:

```
[ec2-user@ip-10-203-10-38 ~]$ sudo yum install -y httpd >/dev/null
[ec2-user@ip-10-203-10-38 ~]$ sudo service httpd start
Starting httpd: httpd: apr_sockaddr_info_get() failed for ip-10-203-10-38
```

```
httpd: Could not reliably determine the server's fully qualified domain
name, using 127.0.0.1 for ServerName
                                                         [  OK  ]

[ec2-user@ip-10-203-10-38 ~]$ cat <<EOF | sudo tee -a /usr/local/bin/
sign.rb >/dev/null
> require 'base64'
> require 'openssl'
> require 'digest/sha1'
> bucket = ENV['AWS_BUCKET']
> local_ip = %x[curl -s http://169.254.169.254/latest/meta-data/local-
ipv4]
> policy_document = <<-EOS
> {"expiration": "2016-01-01T00:00:00Z",
>   "conditions": [
>     ["starts-with", "\$key", "uploads/"],
>     {"bucket": "#{bucket}"},
>     {"acl": "public-read"},
>     {"success_action_redirect": "http://#{local_ip}/"},
>     ["starts-with", "\$Content-Type", "image/jpeg"]
>   ]
> }
> EOS
>
> policy = Base64.encode64(policy_document).gsub("\n","")
> aws_secret_key = ENV['AWS_SECRET_KEY']
> signature = Base64.encode64(
>     OpenSSL::HMAC.digest(
>         OpenSSL::Digest::Digest.new('sha1'),
>         aws_secret_key, policy)
>     ).gsub("\n","")
>
> puts "Local IP: #{local_ip}"
> puts "Base64: #{policy}"
> puts "Signature: #{signature}"
> EOF
```

The server is now configured as a basic Apache server with our ruby script that will sign our request. To do this, we must run it with the right environment variables:

```
[ec2-user@ip-10-203-10-38 ~]$ AWS_SECRET_KEY=mysecret AWS_
BUCKET=31d1f38f-fc88-4899-a382-7a42e9444ec5 ruby /usr/local/bin/sign.rb
Local IP: 10.203.10.38
Base64: alskdjfalsdfj==
Signature: foo=
```

The previous command has given us the information we need for our HTML form, which requires the Base64 encoded policy and the signed string for the policy using our secret key. Use these values for the HTML form making note that the policy as well as the form include the IP of the instance as part of its authorization criteria:

```
[ec2-user@ip-10-203-10-38 ~]$ sudo rm -rf /var/www/html/index.html; cat
<<EOF | sudo tee -a /var/www/html/index.html >/dev/null
> <?xml version="1.0" encoding="UTF-8" ?>
> <html>
> <head>
>   <title>upload</title>
> </head>
> <body>
>     <form action="http://31d1f38f-fc88-4899-a382-7a42e9444ec5.
s3.amazonaws.com/" method="post" enctype="multipart/form-data">
>       <input type="hidden" name="key" value="uploads/\${filename}">
>       <input type="hidden" name="AWSAccessKeyId" value="myaccesskey">
>       <input type="hidden" name="acl" value="public-read">
>       <input type="hidden" name="success_action_redirect"
value="http://10.203.10.38/">
>       <input type="hidden" name="policy" value="alskdjfalsdfj==">
>       <input type="hidden" name="signature" value="foo=">
>       <input type="hidden" name="Content-Type" value="image/jpeg">
>
>       File to upload to S3:
>       <input name="file" type="file">
>       <br>
>       <input type="submit" value="Upload File to S3">
>     </form>
> </body>
> </html>
> EOF
```

If we browse to the instance now, we will be greeted with an upload script. The form and its policy are configured to only allow images (as configured through a content-type header check). Upload any JPEG image and when it is complete, you will be redirected back to your upload script. You can verify the upload was successful by manually checking your S3 bucket.

All Buckets / 31d1f38f-fc88-4899-a382-7a42e9444ec5 / uploads			
Name	Storage Class	Size	Last Modified
021 - 4T9VAvZ.png	Standard	42.8 KB	Thu Jan 01 21:15:58 GMT-600

Summary

In this chapter, we touched on a few examples demonstrating how to handle data uploaded from an end user. Combining these patterns with previous and upcoming patterns will help us come up with robust and inventive solutions with minimal side effects. In the write proxy pattern, we created an FTP server to handle the authorization and shifting of the data from the instance into S3, with a web front-end to allow retrieval later. We then moved to the storage index pattern, which allowed us to optimize the end users' experience at the web front-end by utilizing a metadata store, resulting in a much quicker response and addition of some future search abilities. We then moved to the direct object upload pattern, which removed the need for any pre-processing of the data and allowed us to upload directly into S3 from an HTTP server using the S3 POST method.

In the next chapter, we will move to databases and discuss patterns on creating resilient database and data stores.

7
Patterns for Databases

It has been stated throughout this book that it mostly aims towards web applications in general, and with web applications come databases. There are many shapes and sizes of databases, from relational to non-relational, and this chapter will focus on relational databases. Books of all shapes from authors of all backgrounds have covered databases; so we will try not to beat the dead horse too much in this chapter, but some of those topics are still relevant when moving into a Cloud-backed infrastructure like AWS.

In a traditional web application, there is the front-end instance (typically the user interface), and the backend database instance. In larger and more complex systems, there are many more systems but they all will interact with one or more databases. These non-database systems can be easily architected to be highly available and are generally cheap to scale out when the load becomes high (cheap in this case means that it can be done either by an automated process or has very little effort involved in distributing work).

Databases, on the other hand, require quite a bit of forethought, architecture, planning, and resources to scale. It is not very likely that a database can be optimized or modified without downstream effects on users and systems. Almost every reader, during normal web activity, has likely encountered the dreaded error: **Database Error: Unable to connect to the database: Could not connect to MySQL**.

There are countless issues that can cause this, but thankfully there are just as many patterns and software offerings to help mitigate this downtime. Most patterns here are common to any high availability pattern in the way that the core is based on replication and fail-over.

It should be noted that AWS offers an SLA governance on their RDS, which takes care of most of the common system administration woes such as uptime and availability. It should also be noted that from an operations perspective, RDS is designed to alleviate cost in general. Typically, running a database instance from RDS is much faster to start as it requires little system information and allows creation through the UI. The database instance is also slightly cheaper than running a dedicated EC2 instance, and can be configured to allow automatic security patches. The RDS service does not solve the scalability problem as there is no way to create data shards or small optimization tweaks such as caching. This chapter will cover a few of the patterns that touch on these issues. These will be:

- Database replication pattern
- Read replica pattern
- In-memory cache pattern
- Sharding write pattern

Database replication pattern

The first pattern we will discuss will cover fault tolerance. To maintain zero-downtime to an end user will be a master-client configuration with full replication of data. It is one thing to have a backup of the actual data, but it is important to be able to continue to serve requests even if the data center hosting the instance experiences issues or upgrades, and causes a termination. Consider another scenario in which the database requires system-level updates that would cause it to not be available.

This could be alleviated by having a separate up-to-date instance in a different availability zone. We will first create our master and prepare it to be a MySQL master instance. Launch an EC2 instance from the AWS Linux AMI and SSH into it when it is ready:

```
$ sudo yum install -y mysql mysql-server >/dev/null 2>&1

$ sudo sed -i.bak 's/\[mysqld\]/[mysqld] \nlog-bin=mysql-bin\nserver-id=1/g' /etc/my.cnf

$ sudo service mysqld start >/dev/null 2>&1

$ mysqladmin -u root password 'abc1234!'

$ cat <<EOF | mysql -uroot -pabc1234\!

GRANT SELECT, PROCESS, REPLICATION CLIENT, REPLICATION SLAVE, RELOAD ON *.*  TO 'repl' IDENTIFIED BY 'slavepass';

GRANT ALL ON *.* TO 'root'@'%' IDENTIFIED BY 'abc1234!';

FLUSH PRIVILEGES;

FLUSH TABLES WITH READ LOCK;
```

```
SHOW MASTER STATUS;
UNLOCK TABLES;
EOF
File     Position        Binlog_Do_DB     Binlog_Ignore_DB
mysql-bin.000003         637
```

This instance is now configured as a master and will allow a slave instance to replicate from it using a `repl` user. We will now configure the slave. It is important to make note of the information from the output from the command SHOW MASTER STATUS; under **File Position** and **Binlog_Do_DB**, as we will need them in the slave configuration. Launch another EC2 instance from the AWS Linux AMI into a different geographical availability zone and SSH into it when it is ready (please note that some items may require change based on your configuration and will be in bold).

 It is important to note that the master database instance must be configured with appropriate security groups to allow inbound connections from the slave instance. This will be true for all examples in this chapter.

```
$ sudo yum install -y mysql mysql-server >/dev/null 2>&1
$ sudo sed -i.bak 's/\[mysqld\]/[mysqld] \nlog-bin=mysql-bin\nserver-
id=2/g' /etc/my.cnf
$ sudo service mysqld start >/dev/null 2>&1
$ mysqladmin -u root password 'abc1234!'
$ cat <<EOF | mysql -uroot -pabc1234\!
CHANGE MASTER TO MASTER_HOST='10.203.30.61', MASTER_USER='repl', MASTER_
PASSWORD='slavepass', MASTER_LOG_FILE='mysql-bin.000003', MASTER_LOG_
POS=637;
start slave;
EOF
$ mysql -uroot -pabc1234\! -e 'show slave status\G' | grep Slave_IO_State
            Slave_IO_State: Waiting for master to send event
```

The final command shows the state `Waiting for master to send event`, which means it is properly configured and ready to replicate. We will now create a database, table, and some data, and verify that it replicates to the slave. SSH back into the master instance:

```
$ cat <<EOF | mysql -uroot -pabc1234\!
create database mydb;
use mydb;
```

```
create table people (
id INT AUTO_INCREMENT PRIMARY KEY,
firstname varchar(50),
lastname varchar(50)
);
EOF
$ for i in {1..10}; do
   random_text=$(tr -dc a-z0-9 </dev/urandom | tr 0-9 ' \n' | sed 's/^
*//' | fmt | grep -E '[a-z]+\s[a-z]+' | head -n 1)
   first_name=$(echo $random_text | awk '{print $1}')
   last_name=$(echo $random_text | awk '{print $2}')
cat <<EOF | mysql -uroot -pabc1234\! mydb
insert into people (firstname, lastname) values ('$first_name', '$last_
name');
EOF
done
$ mysql -uroot -pabc1234\! mydb -e 'select count(*) from files;'
+----------+
| count(*) |
+----------+
|       10 |
+----------+
```

The previous snippet creates a database `mydb` and a table `people`. It then uses some clever bash to generate random gibberish names to insert into the table. You can see from the final line that there are 10 rows in the database. Let's now verify that it has replicated to the slave. SSH into the slave instance:

```
$ mysql -uroot -pabc1234\! mydb -e 'select count(*) from files;'
+----------+
| count(*) |
+----------+
|       10 |
+----------+
```

For this pattern we are complete, as we now have two database instances with identical data. From an operations perspective, if the master database experienced a failure or needed to be upgraded, all that would need to happen would be to point the application servers to the slave instance. It should be noted that, in this pattern, it is not appropriate to put these instances behind a load balancer of any kind as we have only solved the replication and availability issue. If the instance is needed to handle additional load, a different pattern would need to be applied. Also, if data were written to the master and immediately retrieved, it might not be available from the slave instance. A final point to note is that this is a one-way synchronization from the master to the slave. Data written to the slave will not propagate to the master.

Read replica pattern

In the previous database replication pattern, we did a full 1:1 replication of data from the master to a slave, more or less as a backup or failover policy. It might be applicable, however, to use the slave as a read-only instance and use the master as a write or update instance. This would allow us to easily configure multiple replications of the data.

The trick to this one is that it is not subject to traditional load-balancing algorithms. If we configure the slaves as read-only instances, then we cannot allow applications to attempt any write executions. To do this, we will use a software on the master called MySQL proxy with a custom proxy script. This script will inspect the execution and determine what instance to issue the command to. The master will receive write commands and the slaves will receive read commands. There are other ways to handle this, and it could be done with other proxy softwares such as HAproxy, or even cluster management tools such as MySQL Fabric or Galera.

 More information on MySQL Fabric can be found at `http://www.mysql.com/products/enterprise/fabric.html`. Additional information on Galera can be found at `http://galeracluster.com/products/`.

First, we will configure MySQL proxy on the master instance created in the previous pattern. In the previous pattern, however, we did not configure the slave to allow connections from the master. Since MySQL proxy is running on the master, we need to allow it to issue read only, or SELECT statements from the master instance. SSH into the slave instance:

```
$ mysql -uroot -pabc1234\! -e "GRANT SELECT ON *.* TO
'root'@'10.203.30.61' IDENTIFIED BY 'abc1234\!';"
```

Now the master can connect to the slave, so SSH into the master instance and install MySQL proxy (provided by EPEL) and download a copy of the `rw-splitting.lua` script into `/usr/local/bin`:

```
$ sudo yum install -y http://dl.fedoraproject.org/pub/epel/6/x86_64/
mysql-proxy-0.8.5-1.el6.x86_64.rpm >/dev/null 2>&1
```

```
$ curl -s https://raw.githubusercontent.com/drmingdrmer/mysql-proxy-xp/
master/lib/rw-splitting.lua | sudo tee -a /usr/local/bin/rw-splitting.lua
>/dev/null 2>&1
```

```
$ sudo sed -i.bak 's/#proxy-lua-script =.*/proxy-lua-script = \/usr\/
local\/bin\/rw-splitting.lua/g' /etc/mysql-proxy.cnf
```

Next, we will configure MySQL proxy to know where the read-write instance lives, or in this case `10.203.30.61`:

```
$ sudo sed -i.bak 's/proxy-backend-addresses =.*/proxy-backend-addresses
= 10.203.30.61:3306/g' /etc/mysql-proxy.cnf
```

Now we must configure the proxy to know where the read-only instance is, or in this case `10.203.30.60`:

```
$ sudo sed -i.bak 's/#proxy-read-only-backend-addresses =.*/proxy-read-
only-backend-addresses = 10.203.30.60:3306/g' /etc/mysql-proxy.cnf
```

```
$ sudo service mysql-proxy start
```

```
Starting mysql-proxy:                                    [  OK  ]
```

Finally, we must prove that our splitting actually works. Note, however, that it might take a few moments or even a few minutes for MySQL proxy to pick up the read-only instance and allow it to be used as such:

```
$ mysql  -uroot -pabc1234\! -h127.0.0.1 -P3307 mydb -e 'select @@
hostname;'
+------------------+
| @@hostname       |
+------------------+
| ip-10-203-30-60  |
+------------------+
$ mysql  -uroot -pabc1234\! -h127.0.0.1 -P3307 mydb -e ' insert into
files (firstname, lastname) values ("asdf", "foo"); select @@hostname;'
+------------------+
| @@hostname       |
+------------------+
| ip-10-203-30-61  |
+------------------+
```

What we have done now is to actually optimize the replication process, to be useful to the application layer that sits on top of the database. The only difference to the application user is that we are using the port 3307 for MySQL proxy. If we wanted this to be truly invisible to other services and systems, we would place the proxy on its own instance on port 3306 and give that information to the application layer. However, this does not resolve the issue of synchronization lag. If the application wrote data and immediately retrieved it, there exists potential for the data to not be immediately available.

Software such as the previously mentioned Galera claims to reduce this issue. However, there are other ways to configure the database to scale outwards without synchronization lag, which will be discussed in the final sharding write pattern. This pattern is now complete.

In-memory cache pattern

While it is important to create a database in which the data is highly available, there are other optimizations possible, depending on the structure. If an application is very read-heavy but does not write very often, it might make sense to use a read-only database with splitting, as designed in the previous pattern. It might also serve the user or consuming system to cache the data so that it does not have to be retrieved on every request.

Consider an application that uses pagination to display information to a user. A typical query might look like `SELECT * FROM products WHERE category=23 LIMIT 50 OFFSET 1000;`. At first glance, this might be acceptable, but for this particular query, the application will execute and retrieve the first 1000 rounds, discard them, and then return the next 50 rows. The retrieval of the 1000 would be a waste of time and resources on data that is changing at a very quick rate. This query will degrade over time as the system continues to grow.

A simple way to offset this cost would be to cache the results wherever possible. There is a downstream effect, however, in that the application must handle this logic; so it is not a transparent optimization to the dependent systems. A typical way to handle this would be to use a fast key-value store such as Redis, for results that have already been computed. From the application perspective, the logic would be as simple as checking the cache for the data, and either using it or doing a database lookup if nothing was found.

We will show a simple example for this using the same pattern as before. The first thing we will do is create a Redis store. You may use the steps from the previous state sharing pattern to do this.

Once the Redis store is configured, we will configure the MySQL database. If you are using one of the previous patterns to create a database, you may skip this section. However, note that there is an addition of a new column in the `files` table named `about` that will be required to follow along. Otherwise, launch an EC2 instance from the AWS Linux AMI and SSH into it when it is ready:

```
$ sudo yum install -y mysql mysql-server >/dev/null 2>&1
$ sudo service mysqld start >/dev/null 2>&1
$ mysqladmin -u root password 'abc1234!'
$ cat <<EOF | mysql -uroot -pabc1234\!
create database mydb;
use mydb;
create table files (
id INT AUTO_INCREMENT PRIMARY KEY,
firstname varchar(50),
lastname varchar(50),
about varchar(1024)
);
EOF
```

Now that the database is configured, we will use the handy bash code from previous snippets to generate and insert random data into it:

```
$ for i in {1..10}; do
  # generate random strings space separated
  random_text=$(tr -dc a-z0-9 </dev/urandom | tr 0-9 ' \n' | sed 's/^
*//' | fmt | grep -E '[a-z]+\s[a-z]+' | head -n 1)

  first_name=$(echo $random_text | awk '{print $1}')
  last_name=$(echo $random_text | awk '{print $2}')

  # generate a random 1024 character string to fill the 'about' col
  about=$(cat /dev/urandom | tr -dc 'a-zA-Z0-9' | fold -w 1024 | head -n
1)

cat <<EOF | mysql -uroot -pabc1234\! mydb
```

```
insert into files (firstname, lastname, about) values ('$first_name',
'$last_name', '$about');
EOF
done
$ mysql -uroot -pabc1234\! mydb -e 'select count(*) from files;' #verify
+----------+
| count(*) |
+----------+
|       10 |
+----------+
```

Now that we have some random data in the database, we will write a PHP application to utilize our cache. The index page will query the files table for names, and create links to a page that displays the information from the about column for that person. We will store this about information into Redis, with the key being their lastname. As a hash, it might resemble:

```
{
    "Young" => "The Author",
    "Smith" => "Some guy"
}
```

If Redis has not cached the about information, we will query the database and then store it into Redis. First, let's set up php 5.5 on our machine:

```
$ sudo yum install -y php55 php55-pecl-redis php55-mysqlnd >/dev/null
2>&1
$ sudo service httpd start
                                        [  OK  ]
```

Now that PHP is set up, we will create our index page that queries MySQL for files. Save this into file /var/www/html/index.php;

```php
<?php
    $redis=new Redis();
    $redis_connected= $redis->connect('127.0.0.1', 6379);
    if(!$redis_connected) {
        die( "Cannot connect to redis server.\n" );
    }
```

```
$mysql_conn = mysql_connect('localhost', 'root', 'abc1234!')
    or die('Could not connect: ' . mysql_error());
mysql_select_db('mydb') or die('Could not select database');

$query = "SELECT firstname, lastname FROM files";
$result = mysql_query($query) or die('Query failed: ' . mysql_
error());
while ($line = mysql_fetch_array($result, MYSQL_ASSOC)) {
    $lastname=$line['lastname'];
    $firstname=$line['firstname'];
    echo "<a href=\"about.php?lname=$lastname\">$firstname $lastname</
a><br/>";
}
?>
```

If you were to browse to your EC2 instance via a web browser, you would be greeted with a list of gibberish names similar to the following screenshot:

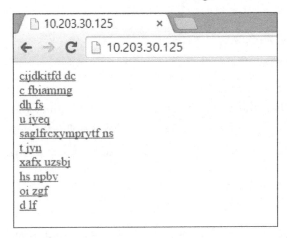

The links will not work until we create the about page. Create a new file at /var/www/html/about.php that contains:

```
<?php
$redis=new Redis();
$redis_connected= $redis->connect('127.0.0.1', 6379);
if(!$redis_connected) {
    // some other code to handle connection problem
    die( "Cannot connect to redis server.\n" );
}

$mysql_conn = mysql_connect('localhost', 'root', 'abc1234!')
```

```
    or die('Could not connect: ' . mysql_error());
mysql_select_db('mydb') or die('Could not select database');

$lname = htmlspecialchars($_GET["lname"]);
$about = '';
$source = '';
if ($redis->exists($lname)) {
  $about = $redis->get($lname);
  $source = "Redis";
} else {
  $query = "SELECT * FROM files WHERE lastname='$lname'";
  $result = mysql_query($query) or die('Query failed: ' . mysql_
error());
  $about = mysql_fetch_array($result, MYSQL_ASSOC)['about'];
  $redis->set($lname, $about);
  $source = 'MySQL';
}
echo "[$source] $about";
?>
```

Now if you click any of the links from your EC2 instance, you will be greeted with the information from the corresponding about column as well as the source, either MySQL or Redis. The first time you click one of the names from the index page, the source will show MySQL, as shown in the following screenshot:

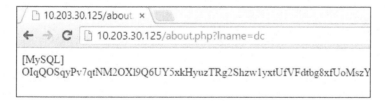

However, if you refresh the about page or click one of the links multiple times, you will see the source change to Redis, as shown in the next screenshot:

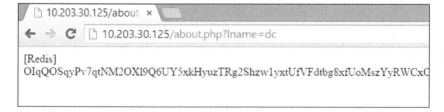

This pattern can be further modified to optimize many portions of a web application in which data caching is applicable. Information that changes often or needs to be at its absolute latest state, should either not be cached or the caching logic should be very carefully architected, so as to not propagate inconsistent or wrong information to the consuming systems or users.

Sharding write pattern

The previous chapter focused a bit on optimization in terms of splitting the query across cloned instances, which would be only part of a true database scalability concern. The database would still have performance concerns, as there is replication lag coupled with a fragile splitting mechanism through the proxy. The best route to take to reduce all of these concerns, is to architect a distributed database from the very beginning.

In the sharding write pattern, we take the previous concepts a bit further in-depth, by not analyzing the query to determine which instance to execute against. Instead, we use a cluster management tool called MySQL Fabric, which was announced by Oracle in early 2014. Fabric provides a single API to create and manage farms (data centers) of databases or even farms of farms of databases. Using this method, we are able to create multiple database instances, and from a Fabric node, group them into many different layouts to achieve high availability.

 More information on MySQL Fabric can be found on their documentation page at http://www.mysql.com/ products/enterprise/fabric.html.

Unlike other patterns, I will not cover the installation steps for configuring a Fabric server in great detail, but will explain the end-goal as though we have an operational cluster. The reason for this is that there is great overhead involved with Fabric that is not relevant to the end-goal.

Sharding as a concept refers to a horizontal partitioning of data within a database. For instance, if we had a table users that contained hundreds of thousands of rows, running searches would take a very long time to complete if all of the data were kept in a single instance. If this database were replicated to another server, then we could expect the replication to never be completed on the slave, as the amount of data would likely be changing at a blazingly fast pace.

The first thing a database administrator might suggest would be to partition the database into partitions, which is a very large architectural concern. Fabric exists to make this management a much smaller concern, as it provides a singular API to create and manage these setups.

Consider the original database example, which conceptually would resemble the following figure:

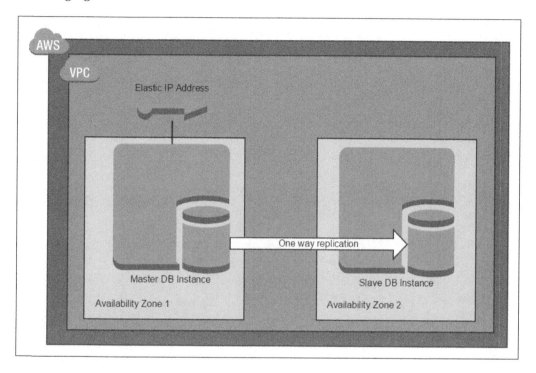

The first improvement we created with the read replica pattern was to increase throughput to the system as a whole by making use of the slave instance as a read-only instance. With Fabric, we open up an entire possibility for improvements right away:

- Create the Fabric node, database, and two shards in a single availability zone
- Create a similar Fabric node, database, and two shards in different availability zones

- Create two Fabric nodes in different availability zones behind a single load balancer

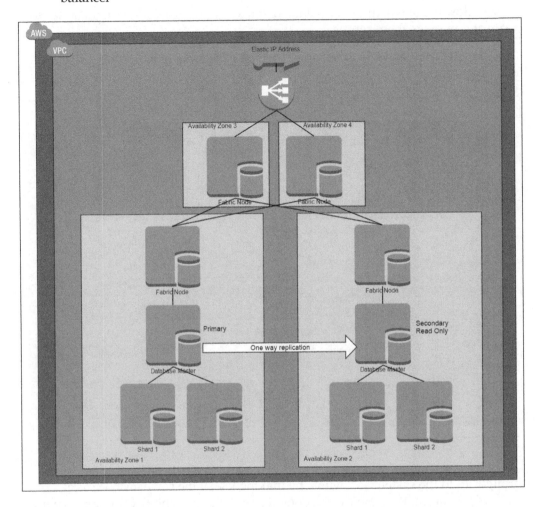

A lot of issues are mitigated if the database is designed as seen in the previous image. From the outside of the database, we have added throughput by:

- Having horizontal nodes behind the load balancer to determine where to execute
- Replicating asynchronously to a read-only database for query optimization
- Partitioning the data into shards for distributed writing

We have also increased our high availability in many ways as well:

- The entry points to the database are load balanced in separate availability zones

- The data from the primary database is replicated into a cluster in a different availability zone

From a database perspective, Fabric takes care of all of the failover for the database. If the primary database experiences any unrecoverable issues, that failure will be picked up from the Fabric management instance above it. For example, if **Availability Zone 1** in the diagram experienced any malfunction, the Fabric node in **Availability Zone 2** could be promoted and changed from read-only to read-write, and vice versa. If either of the availability zones attached to the load balancer experience issues, those issues could be picked up and handled accordingly by a health check directly into the instance via the Fabric API.

One important thing to note if using high availability database software such as Fabric is that the application must be aware of the infrastructure at some level. While the application should not understand the underlying architecture, it cannot interact with Fabric in a transparent manner. For example, MySQL has provided a connector for Fabric but it is not a drop-in replacement for the standard MySQL connector. The methods and calls are slightly different and there are new actions available to a consuming system. The application gains a lot of power through the API, in terms of being able to ask for database instances and layout information from the Fabric API; so it should be constructed carefully to do so.

Summary

In this chapter, we covered a few techniques and patterns for relational databases. In the database replication pattern, we created a MySQL master and client system on EC2 instances to demonstrate one-way replication of data. In the read replica pattern, we further optimized our database access by building on the database replication pattern, by allowing access to the replicated slave instance. We optimized the queries by installing a proxy on the master that decided whether the statements should be executed on the master with write access, or on the slave with read-only access. We then moved on to the In-memory cache pattern, in which we coupled a fast key-value store with our database for read-heavy applications and demonstrated its usage. Lastly, we moved into the sharding write pattern, in which we touched in theory on how to utilize cluster software such as MySQL Fabric to create extremely versatile and optimized clusters of databases that can handle many issues.

In the next chapter, we will discuss how to process batch data throughout systems that scale independently or ad-hoc.

8

Patterns for Data Processing

Throughout the previous chapters, services and infrastructure were described in the traditional fashion of front-end instances that users interact with, middle-tier instances that other systems (including the front-end) interact with, and possibly a back-end instance such as a database. A simple example can be visualized as follows:

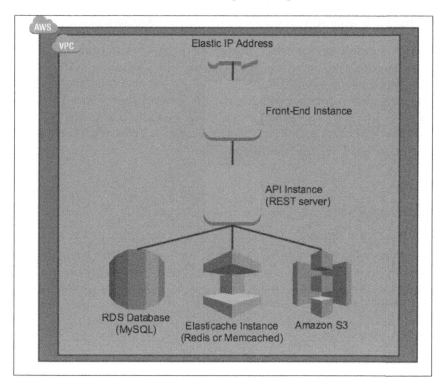

We have described quite a few patterns that help to scale this type of infrastructure at each point, and all of them are valid here; but we can see a bottleneck in the API server. Let's presume that the system as-a-whole is working properly and all is well. Today, however, we have got an unexpected 500% increase in traffic to the front-end server.

We might scale the front-end instances but that would only move the bottleneck to the API instances. Again we could scale the API server, but perhaps the traffic is not utilizing S3 or Redis at all, and most of the traffic is going through to the RDS instance. Scaling out the API server solves the problem, but not in the most optimal fashion in terms of resources. To be as optimal as possible, we would only want to scale in areas that are generating the most work, or by splitting the API server into very specific pieces that do one type of access instead of doing all.

This is a new trend in infrastructure architecture called microservices model. In this architecture, all services live by the core principle of single responsibility. Much like in programming, this means that each part of the infrastructure is responsible for one action and does it well. Instead of having a generic and complex API server, we would have multiple API servers that are independently scalable.

Using metrics, monitoring, and deep health checks, the system can expand and shrink in certain areas ad-hoc. To enable this, we will design our system as a series of workers that get jobs from Amazon's SQS. SQS is a fast and reliable queue provided as a service, meaning Amazon provides an SLA. In a nutshell, this means that you can provide it with data (a message) and retrieve it at any point. Any message taken must be acknowledged in a configurable time, or the service assumes that it was not processed and puts it back into the queue.

 More information on Amazon SQS can be found on their product page at http://aws.amazon.com/sqs/.

There are also non-Amazon options available, such as RabbitMQ, Kafka, ActiveMQ, and others, but deploying these ourselves would require figuring out reliability and redundancy. We will utilize the Amazon-provided service for the following examples and scenarios.

In this chapter we will cover:

- Queuing chain pattern
- Priority queue pattern
- Job observer pattern

Queuing chain pattern

In the queuing chain pattern, we will use a type of publish-subscribe model (pub-sub) with an instance that generates work asynchronously, for another server to pick it up and work with. This is described in the following diagram:

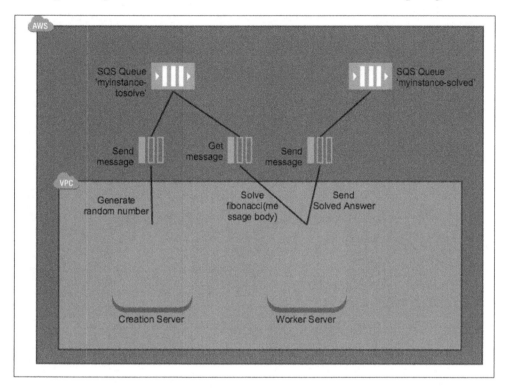

The diagram describes the scenario we will solve, which is solving fibonacci numbers asynchronously. We will spin up a Creator server that will generate random integers, and publish them into an SQS queue **myinstance-tosolve**. We will then spin up a second instance that continuously attempts to grab a message from the queue **myinstance-tosolve**, solves the fibonacci sequence of the numbers contained in the message body, and stores that as a new message in the **myinstance-solved** queue.

Information on the fibonacci algorithm can be found at http://en.wikipedia.org/wiki/Fibonacci_number.

This scenario is very basic as it is the core of the microservices architectural model. In this scenario, we could add as many worker servers as we see fit with no change to infrastructure, which is the real power of the microservices model.

The first thing we will do is create a new SQS queue. From the SQS console select **Create New Queue**.

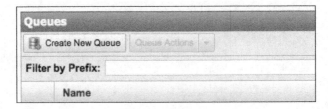

From the **Create New Queue** dialog, enter **myinstance-tosolve** into the **Queue Name** text box and select **Create Queue**.

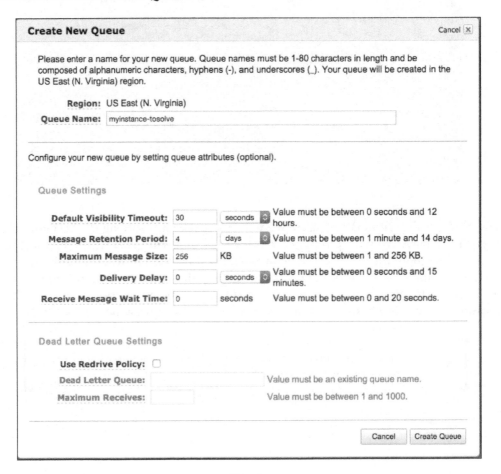

This will create the queue and bring you back to the main SQS console where you can view the queues created. Repeat this process, entering **myinstance-solved** for the second queue name. When complete, the SQS console should list both the queues.

In the following code snippets, you will need the URL for the queues. You can retrieve them from the SQS console by selecting the appropriate queue, which will bring up an information box. The queue URL is listed as **URL** in the following screenshot:

Next, we will launch a creator instance, which will create random integers and write them into the **myinstance-tosolve** queue via its URL noted previously. From the EC2 console, spin up an instance as per your environment from the AWS Linux AMI. Once it is ready, SSH into it (note that `acctarn`, `mykey`, and `mysecret` need to be replaced with your actual credentials):

```
[ec2-user@ip-10-203-10-170 ~]$ [[ -d ~/.aws ]] && rm -rf ~/.aws/config ||
mkdir ~/.aws
```

```
[ec2-user@ip-10-203-10-170 ~]$ echo $'[default]\naws_access_key_id=mykey\
naws_secret_access_key=mysecret\nregion=us-east-1' > .aws/config
```

```
[ec2-user@ip-10-203-10-170 ~]$ for i in {1..100}; do
  value=$(shuf -i 1-50 -n 1)
  aws sqs send-message \
    --queue-url https://queue.amazonaws.com/acctarn/myinstance-tosolve \
    --message-body ${value} >/dev/null 2>&1
done
```

Once the snippet completes, we should have 100 messages in the **myinstance-tosolve** queue, ready to be retrieved.

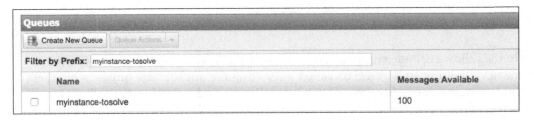

Now that those messages are ready to be picked up and solved, we will spin up a new EC2 instance: again as per your environment from the AWS Linux AMI. Once it is ready, SSH into it (note that acctarn, mykey, and mysecret need to be valid and set to your credentials):

```
[ec2-user@ip-10-203-10-169 ~]$ [[ -d ~/.aws ]] && rm -rf ~/.aws/config ||
mkdir ~/.aws
[ec2-user@ip-10-203-10-169 ~]$ echo $'[default]\naws_access_key_id=mykey\
naws_secret_access_key=mysecret\nregion=us-east-1' > .aws/config
[ec2-user@ip-10-203-10-169 ~]$ sudo yum install -y ruby-devel gcc >/dev/
null 2>&1
[ec2-user@ip-10-203-10-169 ~]$ sudo gem install json >/dev/null 2>&1


[ec2-user@ip-10-203-10-169 ~]$ cat <<EOF | sudo tee -a /usr/local/bin/
fibsqs >/dev/null 2>&1
#!/bin/sh
while [ true ]; do
  function fibonacci {
    a=1
    b=1
    i=0
```

```
    while [ \$i -lt \$1 ]
    do
      printf "%d\n" \$a
      let sum=\$a+\$b
      let a=\$b
      let b=\$sum
      let i=\$i+1
    done
  }


  message=\$(aws sqs receive-message --queue-url https://queue.amazonaws.
com/acctarn/myinstance-tosolve)
  if [[ -n \$message ]]; then
    body=\$(echo \$message | ruby -e "require 'json'; p JSON.parse(gets)
['Messages'][0]['Body']" | sed 's/"//g')
    handle=\$(echo \$message | ruby -e "require 'json'; p JSON.
parse(gets)['Messages'][0]['ReceiptHandle']" | sed 's/"//g')
    aws sqs delete-message --queue-url https://queue.amazonaws.com/
acctarn/myinstance-tosolve --receipt-handle \$handle
    echo "Solving '\${body}'."
    solved=\$(fibonacci \$body)
    parsed_solve=\$(echo \$solved | sed 's/\n/ /g')
    echo "'\${body}' solved."
    aws sqs send-message --queue-url https://queue.amazonaws.com/acctarn/
myinstance-solved --message-body "\${parsed_solve}"
  fi
  sleep 1
done
EOF


[ec2-user@ip-10-203-10-169 ~]$ sudo chown ec2-user:ec2-user /usr/local/
bin/fibsqs && chmod +x /usr/local/bin/fibsqs
```

There will be no output from this code snippet yet, so now let's run the `fibsqs` command we created. This will continuously poll the **myinstance-tosolve** queue, solve the fibonacci sequence for the integer, and store it into the **myinstance-solved** queue:

```
[ec2-user@ip-10-203-10-169 ~]$ fibsqs
Solving '48'.
'48' solved.
{
    "MD5OfMessageBody": "73237e3b7f7f3491de08c69f717f59e6",
    "MessageId": "a249b392-0477-4afa-b28c-910233e7090f"
}
Solving '6'.
'6' solved.
{
    "MD5OfMessageBody": "620b0dd23c3dddbac7cce1a0d1c8165b",
    "MessageId": "9e29f847-d087-42a4-8985-690c420ce998"
}
```

While this is running, we can verify the movement of messages from the **tosolve** queue into the **solved** queue by viewing the **Messages Available** column in the SQS console.

Queues		
Create New Queue Queue Actions ▾		
Filter by Prefix: myinstance		
	Name	**Messages Available**
☐	myinstance-solved	20
☐	myinstance-tosolve	80

This means that the worker virtual machine is in fact doing work, but we can prove that it is working correctly by viewing the messages in the **myinstance-solved** queue. To view messages, right click on the **myinstance-solved** queue and select **View/Delete Messages**.

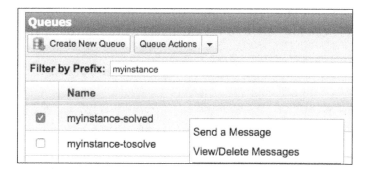

If this is your first time viewing messages in SQS, you will receive a warning box that displays the impact of viewing messages in a queue. Select **Start polling for Messages**.

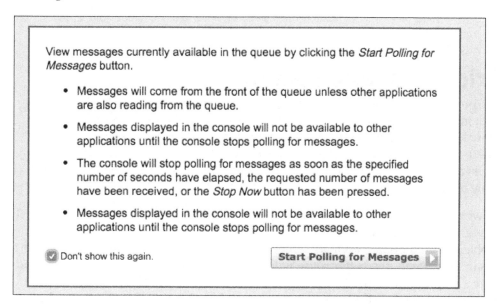

From the **View/Delete Messages in myinstance-solved** dialog, select **Start Polling for Messages**. We can now see that we are in fact working from a queue.

View/Delete Messages in myinstance-solved	
View up to: 100 messages	Poll queue for: 30 seconds

Delete	Body
☐	1 1 2 3 5 8 13 21 34 55 89 144 233 377 610 987 1597 2584
☐	1 1 2 3 5 8 13 21 34 55 89 144 233 377 610 987 1597 2584
☐	1 1 2 3 5 8 13
☐	1 1 2 3 5 8 13 21 34 55 89 144 233 377 610 987 1597 2584

Priority queue pattern

The previous queuing chain pattern is a great example of how to begin working with independent systems in a complex setup. Using the same example, we can show how to give priority to queues using third-party tools. Imagine a system where the workers might have multiple queues to work from. You can scale the worker systems independently by dedicating some instances to one queue and some instances to the other.

However, the problem in doing so is that you will have duplicate logic across both sets of instances. Using the previous example, all workers would still solve the problem with the same fibonacci algorithm but we will have to manage two sets of instances. Instead, the better route would be to assign a weight to the queues and have a single pool of instances assigned to all the queues. This would mean that you must only manage a single set of resources and let the instances determine how to grab from the queues.

This logic of assigning weights is custom but luckily it is not a unique problem and there are multiple third-party solutions available to make this much easier. This example can be visualized as follows:

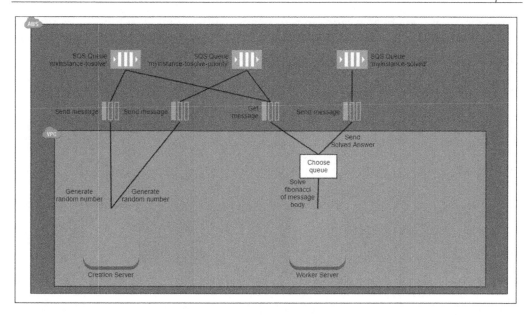

In the diagram, you can see that not much has changed throughout the system as a whole, except that the creator machine will generate random numbers into a new queue **myinstance-tosolve-priority.** The worker instance will now have to determine which queue to pick from, before solving the problem and submitting the answer as before. With this setup, we are very flexible with the worker machine and could spin up as many as we wished without having to modify any system or tie it to a specific input queue.

Before we start, if you are following along then first terminate the running worker instance created in the previous pattern from the EC2 console. Next, ensure that the **myinstance-solved** queue has no messages. This will help us to make sure that this example is behaving as expected. To do this, from the SQS console, right click the **myinstance-solved** queue and select **View/Delete Messages** as demonstrated previously.

From the **View/Delete Messages in myinstance-solved** dialog, set the **View up to:** text box to a high number and then select **Start Polling for Messages** as before. Select the checkbox next to each message and select **Delete Messages**.

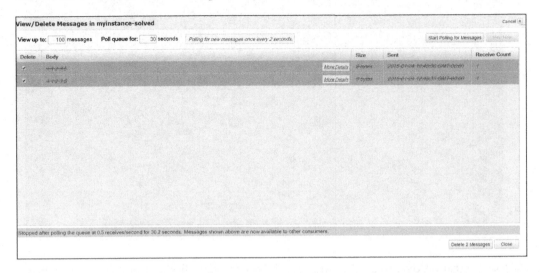

From the new **Delete Messages** confirmation dialog, select **Yes, Delete Checked Messages**. The messages are now gone from the queue.

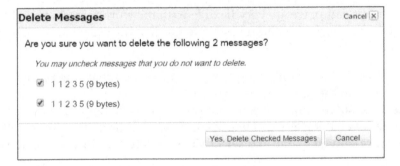

To start, let's create a new queue named **myinstance-tosolve-priority**. You may create this the same way as we did in the previous pattern. Once it has been created, make note of its **URL** from the SQS console. We will now generate random numbers equally into both queues. You may either modify the creator instance from the previous pattern or launch a new instance from the EC2 console as per your environment, and SSH into it when it is ready (note that acctarn, mykey, and mysecret need to be valid):

```
[ec2-user@ip-10-203-10-79 ~]$ [[ -d ~/.aws ]] && rm -rf ~/.aws/config ||
mkdir ~/.aws
```

```
[ec2-user@ip-10-203-10-79 ~]$ echo $'[default]\naws_access_key_id=mykey\
naws_secret_access_key=mysecret\nregion=us-east-1' > .aws/config


[ec2-user@ip-10-203-10-79 ~]$ for i in {1..100}; do
  value=$(shuf -i 1-50 -n 1)
  aws sqs send-message \
    --queue-url https://queue.amazonaws.com/acctarn/myinstance-tosolve \
    --message-body ${value} >/dev/null 2>&1
done


[ec2-user@ip-10-203-10-79 ~]$ for i in {1..100}; do
  value=$(shuf -i 1-50 -n 1)
  aws sqs send-message \
    --queue-url https://queue.amazonaws.com/acctarn/myinstance-tosolve-
priority \
    --message-body ${value} >/dev/null 2>&1
done
```

At this point, we have messages ready in both **myinstance-tosolve** and **myinstance-tosolve-priority** queues. We will create a new worker that uses a third-party piece of software called Shoryuken, to set weights on SQS queues and retrieve messages based on an internal algorithm.

 More information on Shoryuken can be found on its GitHub page at https://github.com/phstc/shoryuken.

Next, launch an instance via the EC2 console from the AWS Linux AMI as per your environment and SSH into it when it is ready (note that acctarn, mykey, and mysecret need to be valid):

```
[ec2-user@ip-10-203-10-82 ~]$ [[ -d ~/.aws ]] && rm -rf ~/.aws/config ||
mkdir ~/.aws
[ec2-user@ip-10-203-10-82 ~]$ echo $'[default]\naws_access_key_id=mykey\
naws_secret_access_key=mysecret\nregion=us-east-1' > .aws/config
[ec2-user@ip-10-203-10-82 ~]$ cat <<EOF | sudo tee -a /usr/local/bin/
fibsqs >/dev/null 2>&1
#!/bin/sh
function fibonacci {
  a=1
```

```
    b=1
    i=0

    while [ \$i -lt \$1 ]
    do
      printf "%d\n" \$a
      let sum=\$a+\$b
      let a=\$b
      let b=\$sum
      let i=\$i+1
    done
}


number="\$1"


solved=\$(fibonacci \$number)
parsed_solve=\$(echo \$solved | sed 's/\n/ /g')
aws sqs send-message --queue-url https://queue.amazonaws.com/acctarn/
myinstance-solved --message-body "\${parsed_solve}"
exit 0
EOF
[ec2-user@ip-10-203-10-82 ~]$ sudo chown ec2-user:ec2-user /usr/local/
bin/fibsqs && sudo chmod +x /usr/local/bin/fibsqs
```

The preceding script is slightly different from the one in the previous example, it takes a parameter (the number to solve) as input. We will be calling it from a ruby script that uses shoryuken to get the messages. We will install the prerequisites next:

```
[ec2-user@ip-10-203-10-82 ~]$ sudo yum install -y libxml2 libxml2-devel
libxslt libxslt-devel gcc ruby-devel >/dev/null 2>&1
  [ec2-user@ip-10-203-10-82 ~]$ sudo gem install nokogiri -- --use-system-
libraries >/dev/null 2>&1
  [ec2-user@ip-10-203-10-82 ~]$ sudo gem install shoryuken >/dev/null 2>&1
```

We have now installed the shoryuken package but we must configure it. Create a file named config.yml with the contents (note that mykey, and mysecret need to be valid):

```
aws:
  access_key_id:      mykey
  secret_access_key:  mysecret
  region:             us-east-1 # or <%= ENV['AWS_REGION'] %>
```

```
receive_message:
  attributes:
    - receive_count
    - sent_at
concurrency: 25,  # The number of allocated threads to process messages.
Default 25
delay: 25,       # The delay in seconds to pause a queue when it's
empty. Default 0
queues:
  - [myinstance-tosolve-priority, 2]
  - [myinstance-tosolve, 1]
```

With the required configuration file in place, we can now create a ruby script that contains the information to execute messages from the queue. Create a file called worker.rb and give it the contents:

```ruby
class MyWorker
  include Shoryuken::Worker

  shoryuken_options queue: 'myinstance-tosolve', auto_delete: true

  def perform(sqs_msg, body)
    puts "normal: #{body}"
    %x[/usr/local/bin/fibsqs #{body}]
  end
end


class MyFastWorker
  include Shoryuken::Worker

  shoryuken_options queue: 'myinstance-tosolve-priority', auto_delete:
true

  def perform(sqs_msg, body)
    puts "priority: #{body}"
    %x[/usr/local/bin/fibsqs #{body}]
  end
end
```

We are now ready to run this. There will be a lot of output, but we will direct it into a file for later:

```
[ec2-user@ip-10-203-10-82 ~]$ shoryuken -r /home/ec2-user/worker.rb -C /
home/ec2-user/config.yml >output.log
```

Once it has finished running, we will look for the messages in the **myinstance-solved** queue in the SQS console, as described in the previous pattern. Unfortunately, the script won't stop executing once it's done; it will continue to poll for messages. To end it, ensure that there are 200 messages in the **Messages Available** column of the **myinstance-solved** queue in the SQS console.

View/Delete Messages in myinstance-solved	
View up to: 100 messages	Poll queue for: 30 seconds

Delete	Body
☐	1 1 2 3 5 8 13 21 34 55 89 144 233 377 610 987 1597 2584
☐	1 1 2 3 5 8 13 21 34 55 89 144 233 377 610 987 1597 2584
☐	1 1 2 3 5 8 13 21 34 55 89 144 233 377 610 987 1597 2584
☐	1 1 2 3 5 8 13 21

When the queue has all of the expected messages in it, you can cancel the running command. We now know that the fibonacci numbers are still being solved correctly, but let's prove that it gave priority to the **myinstance-tosolve-priority** queue by viewing the output.log file. First, let's parse out the relevant output to show which worker got a job and and the contents of the message body into the log file parsed_output.log:

```
[ec2-user@ip-10-203-10-82 ~]$ cat output.log | grep -E
'^normal:|^priority:' >parsed_output.log
```

Now, using an editor of your choice, count the duplicated lines. This will tell us how many messages were pulled from the **myinstance-tosolve** queue (or **normal** in the output) and how many were pulled from the **myinstance-tosolve-priority** queue (or **priority** in the output). Repeat the counting. My output showed in this order: 10 priority, 10 normal, 15 priority, 10 normal, 3 priority, 1 normal, 20 priority, 1 normal, 2 priority, 10 normal, 11 priority, 2 normal, 2 priority, 1 normal, 37 priority, 65 normal. Since both of these add up to 100 individually and 200 total, my basic math skills are up to par. As you can see from the pattern, priority messages were in fact given priority while normal messages were not fully neglected, but were fewer in between until the priority queue had emptied.

Job observer pattern

The previous two patterns show a very basic understanding of passing messages around a complex system, so that components (machines) can work independently from each other. While they are a good starting place, the system as a whole could improve if it were more autonomous. Given the previous example, we could very easily duplicate the worker instance if either one of the SQS queues grew large, but using the Amazon-provided CloudWatch service we can automate this process. Using CloudWatch similar to the *Scale out pattern* from *Chapter 2, Basic Patterns,* we might end up with a system that resembles the following diagram:

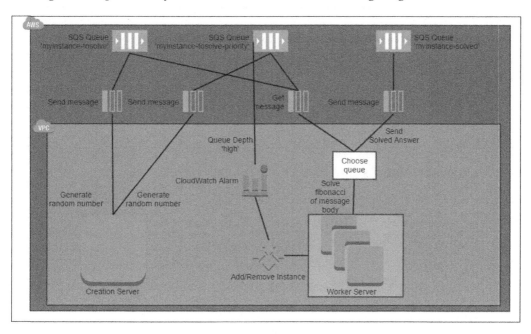

For this pattern, we will not start from scratch but directly from the previous priority queuing pattern. The major difference between the previous diagram and the diagram displayed in the priority queuing pattern is the addition of a CloudWatch alarm on the **myinstance-tosolve-priority** queue, and the addition of an auto scaling group for the worker instances.

The behavior of this pattern is that we will define a depth for our priority queue that we deem too high, and create an alarm for that threshold. If the number of messages in that queue goes beyond that point, it will notify the auto scaling group to spin up an instance. When the alarm goes back to *OK*, meaning that the number of messages is below the threshold, it will scale down as much as our auto scaling policy allows.

Before we start, make sure any worker instances are terminated.

The first thing we should do is create an alarm. From the CloudWatch console in AWS, click **Alarms** on the side bar and select **Create Alarm**.

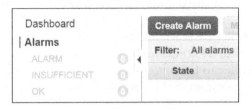

From the new **Create Alarm** dialog, select **Queue Metrics** under **SQS Metrics**.

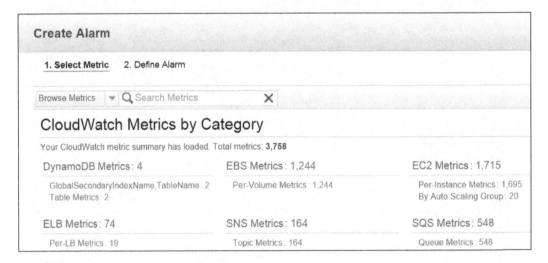

This will bring us to a **Select Metric** section. Type `myinstance-tosolve-priority ApproximateNumberOfMessagesVisible` into the search box and hit *Enter*. Select the checkbox for the only row and select **Next**.

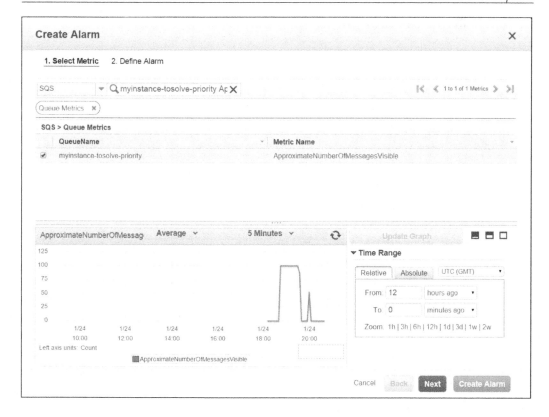

From the **Define Alarm,** make the following changes and then select **Create Alarm**:

1. In the **Name** textbox, give the alarm a unique name.
2. In the **Description** textbox, give the alarm a general description.
3. In the **Whenever** section, set 0 to 1.
4. In the **Actions** section, click **Delete** for the only **Notification**.
5. In the **Period** drop-down, select **1 Minute**.

6. In the **Statistic** drop-down, select **Sum**.

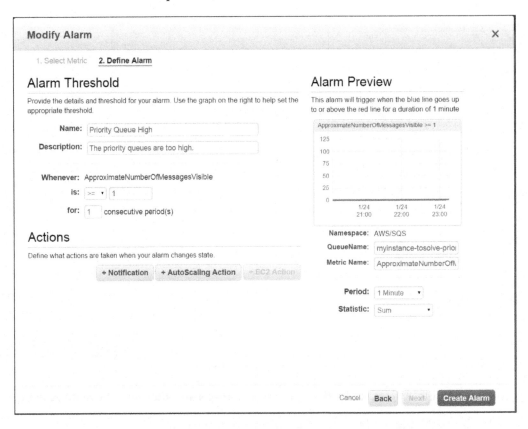

Now that we have our alarm in place, we need to create a launch configuration and auto scaling group that refers this alarm. We have done this in *Chapter 2, Basic Patterns*, so I will not cover it in great detail here.

Create a new launch configuration from the AWS Linux AMI with details as per your environment. However, set the user data to (note that `acctarn`, `mykey`, and `mysecret` need to be valid):

```
#!/bin/bash

[[ -d /home/ec2-user/.aws ]] && rm -rf /home/ec2-user/.aws/config ||
mkdir /home/ec2-user/.aws

echo $'[default]\naws_access_key_id=mykey\naws_secret_access_
key=mysecret\nregion=us-east-1' > /home/ec2-user/.aws/config

chown ec2-user:ec2-user /home/ec2-user/.aws -R

cat <<EOF >/usr/local/bin/fibsqs

#!/bin/sh
```

```
function fibonacci {
  a=1
  b=1
  i=0

  while [ \$i -lt \$1 ]
  do
    printf "%d\n" \$a
    let sum=\$a+\$b
    let a=\$b
    let b=\$sum
    let i=\$i+1
  done
}


number="\$1"


solved=\$(fibonacci \$number)
parsed_solve=\$(echo \$solved | sed 's/\n/ /g')
aws sqs send-message --queue-url https://queue.amazonaws.com/acctarn/
myinstance-solved --message-body "\${parsed_solve}"
exit 0
EOF
chown ec2-user:ec2-user /usr/local/bin/fibsqs
chmod +x /usr/local/bin/fibsqs
yum install -y libxml2 libxml2-devel libxslt libxslt-devel gcc ruby-devel
>/dev/null 2>&1
gem install nokogiri -- --use-system-libraries >/dev/null 2>&1
gem install shoryuken >/dev/null 2>&1
cat <<EOF >/home/ec2-user/config.yml
aws:
  access_key_id:        mykey
  secret_access_key:    mysecret
  region:               us-east-1 # or <%= ENV['AWS_REGION'] %>
  receive_message:
    attributes:
```

```
        - receive_count
        - sent_at
concurrency: 25,   # The number of allocated threads to process messages.
Default 25
delay: 25,         # The delay in seconds to pause a queue when it's
empty. Default 0
queues:
  - [myinstance-tosolve-priority, 2]
  - [myinstance-tosolve, 1]
EOF
cat <<EOF >/home/ec2-user/worker.rb
class MyWorker
  include Shoryuken::Worker

  shoryuken_options queue: 'myinstance-tosolve', auto_delete: true

  def perform(sqs_msg, body)
    puts "normal: #{body}"
    %x[/usr/local/bin/fibsqs #{body}]
  end
end

class MyFastWorker
  include Shoryuken::Worker

  shoryuken_options queue: 'myinstance-tosolve-priority', auto_delete:
true

  def perform(sqs_msg, body)
    puts "priority: #{body}"
    %x[/usr/local/bin/fibsqs #{body}]
  end
end
EOF
chown ec2-user:ec2-user /home/ec2-user/worker.rb /home/ec2-user/config.
yml
screen -dm su - ec2-user -c 'shoryuken -r /home/ec2-user/worker.rb -C /
home/ec2-user/config.yml'
```

Next, create an auto scaling group that uses the launch configuration we just created. The rest of the details for the auto scaling group are as per your environment. However, set it to start with 0 instances and do not set it to receive traffic from a load balancer.

Once the auto scaling group has been created, select it from the EC2 console and select **Scaling Policies**. From here, click **Add Policy** to create a policy similar to the one shown in the following screenshot and click **Create**:

Next, we get to trigger the alarm. To do this, we will again submit random numbers into both the **myinstance-tosolve** and **myinstance-tosolve-priority** queues:

```
[ec2-user@ip-10-203-10-79 ~]$ [[ -d ~/.aws ]] && rm -rf ~/.aws/config ||
mkdir ~/.aws
[ec2-user@ip-10-203-10-79 ~]$ echo $'[default]\naws_access_key_id=mykey\
naws_secret_access_key=mysecret\nregion=us-east-1' > .aws/config

[ec2-user@ip-10-203-10-79 ~]$ for i in {1..100}; do
  value=$(shuf -i 1-50 -n 1)
  aws sqs send-message \
    --queue-url https://queue.amazonaws.com/acctarn/myinstance-tosolve \
    --message-body ${value} >/dev/null 2>&1
done

[ec2-user@ip-10-203-10-79 ~]$ for i in {1..100}; do
  value=$(shuf -i 1-50 -n 1)
  aws sqs send-message \
    --queue-url https://queue.amazonaws.com/acctarn/myinstance-tosolve-
priority \
    --message-body ${value} >/dev/null 2>&1
done
```

After five minutes, the alarm will go into effect and our auto scaling group will launch an instance to respond to it. This can be viewed from the **Scaling History** tab for the auto scaling group in the EC2 console.

 Even though our alarm is set to trigger after one minute, CloudWatch only updates in intervals of five minutes. This is why our wait time was not as short as our alarm.

Our auto scaling group has now responded to the alarm by launching an instance.

Launching an instance by itself will not resolve this, but using the user data from the Launch Configuration, it should configure itself to clear out the queue, solve the fibonacci of the message, and finally submit it to the **myinstance-solved** queue. If this is successful, our **myinstance-tosolve-priority** queue should get emptied out. We can verify from the SQS console as before.

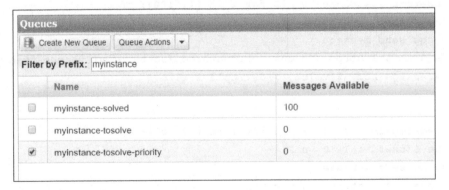

And finally, our alarm in CloudWatch is back to an **OK** status.

We are now stuck with the instance because we have not set any decrease policy. I won't cover this in detail, but to set it, we would create a new alarm that triggers when the message count is a lower number such as 0, and set the auto scaling group to decrease the instance count when that alarm is triggered. This would allow us to scale out when we are over the threshold, and scale in when we are under the threshold. This completes the final pattern for data processing.

Summary

In this chapter, we covered some in-depth techniques on how to split up complex systems into self-contained microservices. In the queuing chain pattern, we walked through creating independent systems that use the Amazon-provided SQS service that solve fibonacci numbers without interacting with each other directly. We then took the topic a bit deeper in the priority queue pattern, and covered creating multiple queues that have implicit weights upon them, so that one queue gets worked from more frequently than the other queue. Lastly, we took the topic even deeper in the job observer pattern, and covered how to tie in auto scaling policies and alarms from the CloudWatch service to scale out when the priority queue gets too deep.

In the next chapter, we will discuss patterns and topics designed to help with the operations and maintenance of infrastructure deployed at AWS.

9
Patterns for Operation and Maintenance

Many of the patterns discussed in this book so far have been focused on very narrow paths through problems encountered in the Cloud, as well as a few areas where it is possible to boost resiliency to different types of service interruptions. In this chapter, we will take a small step back, and focus on a few advanced patterns that many teams have implemented in different forms to solve core operational issues. In this chapter, we will touch on:

- Bootstrap pattern: Dynamically pulling settings or initialization steps on startup.
- Cloud dependency injection pattern: Injecting information to the machine through external means.
- Stack deployment pattern: Deploying entire stacks of applications in a single run.
- Monitoring integration pattern: Centralizing application and system logs along with metrics.
- Web storage archive pattern: Moving and maintaining files from running instances into long-term storage.
- Weighted transition pattern: Transitioning servers to different locations in small portions to mitigate problems.
- Hybrid backup pattern: Using Cloud-storage as a backup for alternate services on premises or in other Cloud locations.

The purpose of the topics in this chapter will be to elaborate on basic patterns and create building blocks of sorts. Combining these patterns with previous patterns will help to create some very unique and dynamic environments. These patterns will also help to separate logic from the virtual machine images themselves, saving time and effort when small tweaks are needed.

Bootstrap pattern

Looking back at the previous stamp pattern, we created an image of a virtual machine at a point where it made many things easier, including scaling out or even making one-time changes to enable the third-party software Vagrant.

A lot of times, the stamp pattern is used to solve the deployment concern of locking an image at an application state. For example, if the team deploys a web page, they might stamp the running instance after the web server has been configured with Apache, SSL, PHP, etc. However, perhaps this server requires SSL so the image is created, or stamped, after the certificate is installed. The even bigger risk is that SSL keys, SSH keys, and so on should never be left on an AMI.

Certificates change and expire over time, so this means that the machine image would become invalid at some point in its lifecycle. The best way to handle this change without having to re-package the entire virtual machine would be to separate the configuration (or certificates) from the machine itself. In the previous scenario, a change to configuration such as the certificate would require fixing the image and re-imaging it, as well as modifying any services or configuration that depend on the previous image, such as launch configurations.

In the bootstrap pattern, we will configure a box as much as possible, but allow it to be configured at startup, dynamically using user data. User data is an AWS concept for startup configuration. For Windows instances, it requires the `EC2Config` utility to be installed and configured, and allows normal command prompt as well as Powershell scripting. For Linux instances, user data uses Bash scripting.

> More detailed information on user-data can be found in the documentation page at `http://docs.aws.amazon.com/AWSEC2/latest/UserGuide/user-data.html`.

However, this pattern is more than just using user data. It does us no good to configure an instance that cannot be changed later, so we will complicate things a bit. In the previous real world example, we packaged the web server with the AMI to lock down versions and made start up times a bit faster, but in this example, we will skip that step and use the user data to install the web server.

However, we will separate the web pages from the instance, so that small changes can be propagated with very little effort. To do this, we will store the HTML in an S3 bucket and have the user-data grab it. This way, if the HTML file needs to change, we can do that without needing to modify downstream services or configuration items.

There are a few prerequisite steps to achieve this. I will create an Amazon S3 bucket named **1ce8b98d-8735-47ff-a9dc-7f4b57820a74**. Remember that buckets need to remain unique, so you need to create a bucket that does not exist. Do this through the S3 console. Once complete, create a file named **index.php** with the following contents and upload it into the bucket we just created:

```php
<?php
  echo "test from PHP via userdata!";
?>
```

Now that the file is there, we need to make sure that the instance has access to it. We will do this through an **Identity and Access Management (IAM)** profile. We will not go into a whole lot of detail on how IAM works in general, but in order to access an S3 bucket, either the bucket should have a policy to allow certain objects to access it, or those objects should have policies that allow them to access the bucket. We will do the latter.

 More information on AWS IAM roles and profiles can be found on the documentation page at http://aws.amazon.com/iam/.

Browse to the IAM **Dashboard,** and then select **Roles**.

From the **Roles** section, select **Create New Role**.

In the **Set Role Name** dialog, name it whatever you choose in the **Role Name** text box. For this example, I will name it **testRole**.

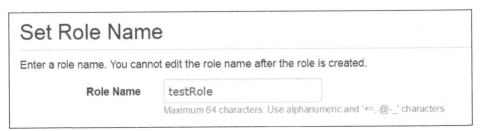

Next, from the **Select Role Type** window, we will click **Select** next to **Amazon EC2** under **AWS Service Roles**. We do this because we want an EC2 instance to access an AWS service, or S3.

We have many options to choose from in the **Set Permissions** window, and the choice is up to the user, dependent on what is being achieved. Sometimes, it is best to select a pre-configured template from **Select Policy Template**. However, it may also be relevant to generate a policy, as that gives some validation and might be helpful when starting out.

I will provide the policy, so we will select **Custom Policy**. Click the newly visible **Select** button.

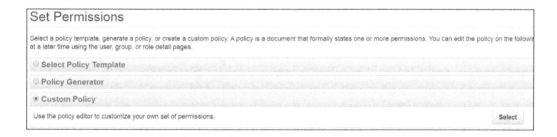

If you encounter a new dropdown for permissions, select **click here** underneath **Inline Policies** section.

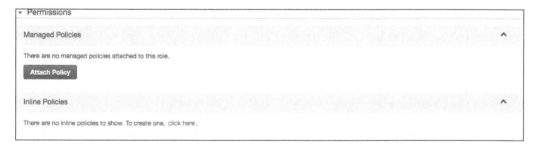

In the new **Set Permissions** pane, enter `1ce8b98d-8735-47ff-a9dc-7f4b57820a74_ GodMode` for **Policy Name**. Paste the following JSON snippet into the **Policy Document** section and click **Next Step**.

```json
{
  "Version": "2012-10-17",
  "Statement": [
    {
      "Sid": "BucketList",
      "Effect": "Allow",
      "Action": [
        "s3:List*"
      ],
      "Resource": [
        "arn:aws:s3:::1ce8b98d-8735-47ff-a9dc-7f4b57820a74"
      ]
    },
    {
      "Sid": "BucketAll",
      "Effect": "Allow",
      "Action": [
        "s3:*"
      ],
      "Resource": [
        "arn:aws:s3:::1ce8b98d-8735-47ff-a9dc-7f4b57820a74/*"
      ]
    }
  ]
}
```

A quick dissection of the above snippet shows that if this policy is applied, it will have the ability to list the bucket we created and also have full access to anything inside of the bucket.

In the **Review** section, click **Create Role**.

We now have a bucket that contains our PHP file, and a policy that will allow us to access it. We will now launch an instance from the AWS Linux AMI as we have many times before. However, during the creation steps from the EC2 console, please ensure that you apply our new `testRole` **IAM role** to the instance as well as paste this into the **User data** section:

```sh
#!/bin/sh
yum groupinstall -y "Web Server" "PHP Support"
aws s3 cp s3://1ce8b98d-8735-47ff-a9dc-7f4b57820a74/index.php /var/
www/html/index.php
service httpd start
```

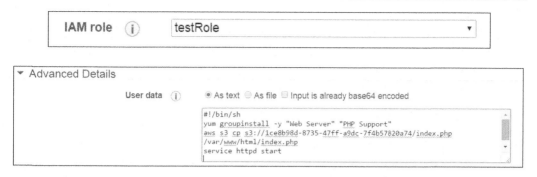

Once the instance has finished launching, and if all steps were carefully followed, then we will be able to access the instance from a web browser and see that the PHP script is usable.

With this pattern, we have succeeded in separating a piece from the instance itself, so that any future changes to the configuration (or in this case the PHP file) does not require any intervention to services or objects downstream. We could even go so far as to create a timer that continuously updates the **/var/www/html** directory with the contents of the bucket. In a more extreme case, we could separate everything entirely and have the user data pull its entire configuration set up from S3 in the form of a bash file. If we went that route, we could separate the user data altogether and make bigger changes to the system through S3 configuration. The beauty of this pattern is that it opens up countless areas for improvement and unique solutions.

Cloud dependency injection pattern

One benefit to the previous bootstrap pattern was that we were able to separate small configurations of the instance at start-up. This allowed us to alleviate some maintenance headaches, such as modifying the web page content on-the-fly. Imagine that the application consists of multiple web servers or even servers with entirely different purposes. For example, the user data we provided for the web server is not relevant to a database instance.

To take this further, we could separate it even further and have a common set of user data across all instances. This user data could go to S3 and get the actual configuration script it needs, whether that is to set it up as a web server or a database server, and run that. To do this, we would need metadata at the start up level to decide what user data to use.

To resolve this, we will make use of the tagging system that AWS provides for nearly all of its services, including EC2 instances. Tags are quite common on instances to provide the ability to see what its purpose is, but it can be utilized much more effectively by the instance itself. In this example, we will create a concept of a role to an instance. The user data will be very generic so that it might never need to be updated, as its only purpose will be to query its tag information, decide what script to retrieve from S3, and run it.

 More information on tagging AWS resources can be found on the documentation page at http://docs.aws.amazon.com/ AWSEC2/latest/UserGuide/Using_Tags.html.

However, there is a prerequisite step. By default, AWS does not allow instances to query their metadata, so we must modify the **IAM role** we created in the previous pattern to allow this. From IAM **Dashboard,** select **Roles** and select the testRole we created. We will create a new policy via the **Create Role Policy** button.

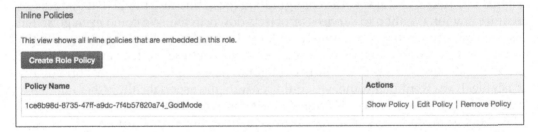

Select **Custom Policy** from the **Set Permissions** window and click the **Select** button. Enter describe-tags into the **Policy Name** text box and paste the following JSON into the **Policy Document** area:

```
{
    "Version": "2012-10-17",
    "Statement": [
      {
        "Sid": "BucketList",
        "Effect": "Allow",
        "Action": "ec2:DescribeTags",
        "Resource": "*"
```

```
        }
    ]
}
```

Once the IAM policy has been created, we are ready to move our original user data into S3. From the S3 dashboard, browse to the `1ce8b98d-8735-47ff-a9dc-7f4b57820a74` bucket we created. Upload the following snippet to a new file named `webserver.sh`:

```sh
#!/bin/sh
yum groupinstall -y "Web Server" "PHP Support"
export AWS_DEFAULT_REGION=us-east-1
aws s3 cp s3://1ce8b98d-8735-47ff-a9dc-7f4b57820a74/index.php /var/
www/html/index.php
service httpd start
```

 It is important to note that creating and uploading bash files requires them to have valid Unix newlines. If you are using a windows computer or any text editor that saves using any other newline scheme, such as the Windows default CRLF, there will be many unpleasant side effects. Please ensure that if this is the case, your editor saves using Unix line endings.

You may notice that it is the user data we used in the previous example.

We are now ready to launch our instance from the EC2 console. During the creation, ensure that you apply `testRole` to the instance and paste the following snippet of code into the user data section:

```bash
#!/bin/bash
function get_tag {
    instance_id=$(curl --silent http://169.254.169.254/latest/meta-data/
instance-id)
    tag=$(aws ec2 describe-tags \
    --filters "Name=resource-type,Values=instance" \
    "Name=resource-id,Values=${instance_id}" \
    "Name=key,Values=$1" \
    | grep Value | awk '{print $2}' | sed 's/"\|,//g')
```

```
}

echo $'#!/bin/sh\nexport AWS_DEFAULT_REGION=us-east-1\n' > /etc/
profile.d/aws.sh

. /etc/profile.d/aws.sh

get_tag 'Role'
ROLE=$tag
export AWS_DEFAULT_REGION=us-east-1
aws s3 cp s3://1ce8b98d-8735-47ff-a9dc-7f4b57820a74/${ROLE}.sh /tmp/
userdata.sh
sh /tmp/userdata.sh >/var/log/custom-userdata.sh 2>&1
```

Finally, make sure that you create a tag Role with the value webserver to make this process work.

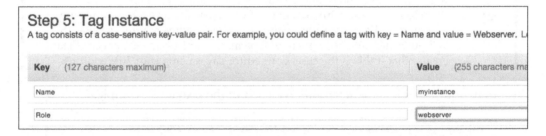

Finish launching this instance and within a few moments it will be accessible just as in the previous example:

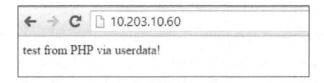

We have now decoupled the user data entirely from our instance. This allows for some very dynamic solutions to common configuration issues and allows you to apply common user data to every Linux instance. This completes the Cloud dependency injection pattern.

Stack deployment pattern

It is quite common to bring up multiple instances at once, either for testing how a system behaves as a whole or even just to reduce errors in the creation process. A new movement in the DevOps community is to treat the infrastructure itself as code. This allows the operations team to view differences between environments, see the current state, and even see what changes will affect what pieces of the environment.

AWS provides this ability through their CloudFormation service. CloudFormation allows an authorized user to deploy almost any AWS object and service, either at once or through tiered set ups using JSON templates. These templates can have input parameters, making them very generic, as well as defining dynamic resources, and producing outputs. These outputs can then be used either to give information to the user or as inputs to another CloudFormation template.

 More information about CloudFormation can be found on their documentation page at `https://aws.amazon.com/cloudformation/`.

In this example, we will use a CloudFormation template to spin up a database server with some sample data in it, as well as a front-end web instance that uses the database server. This will be an all-in-one process that requires very little intervention to show a very limited example of how powerful the CloudFormation service is.

There are, however, a few things to be noted. The template itself is quite large, so we will only be looking at relevant snippets of it to move through the example. The full JSON is provided along with the book. That JSON also may not be relevant to a default AWS environment as it uses a VPC and only contains internal IPs. Though it may not be usable as-is to the reader, it can be used as a template of sorts to try to understand how to tie multiple instances together.

First we will break down a few relevant parts of the JSON we will upload. The general layout of the CloudFormation template that we will use resembles:

```
{
  "AWSTemplateFormatVersion": "2010-09-09",
  "Description": "Full stack template example",
  "Parameters": {
  },
  "Resources": {
  },
  "Outputs": {
  }
}
```

The most important parts of this outline are `Parameters`, `Resources`, and `Outputs`. Within the template, nearly anywhere, you can reference variables as values, arrays, or hashes. This is good when you wish to either remove duplication or want the template to be a bit more generic.

In the `Parameters` section, we will define a few variables such as the `IAM role` to use, the base AMI to use, what subnet to put the instances under, and so on. With parameters, you may either use a default value, allow the value to be specified during the template upload, or use a combination of both. A parameter with a default value might resemble:

```
"Parameters": {
    "AWSAMI": {
      "Default": "ami-146e2a7c",
      "Type": "String",
      "Description": "The AMI ID for the AWS Linux instance."
    }
}
```

In the `Resources` section, we can define nearly any resource as long as it is valid as per CloudFormations' internal validation scheme, which will check for circular dependencies among resources and valid JSON syntax, along with many other checks. You can reference other resources from a resource via a `Fn:GetAttr` call, or from parameters via a `Ref` lookup. There are quite a few functions provided to you to use in CloudFormation, but these are the ones you will find in the template provided with the book. A resource might resemble:

```
"WebInstance": {
    "Type": "AWS::EC2::Instance",
    "Properties": {
      "ImageId": { "Ref": "AWSAMI" },
      "NetworkInterfaces": [
        {
          "GroupSet": [ {
             "Ref": "FirstSecurityGroup"
            } ],
          "AssociatePublicIpAddress": "false",
          "SubnetId": {
            "Ref": "SubnetId"
          }
        }
      ],
      "KeyName": { "Ref": "KeyName" },
      "InstanceType": "t2.micro"
    }
}
```

Lastly, in the Outputs section, we would output anything relevant to a service or the end user, such as DNS entries of instances, load balancers created, or even the instance-ids of the instances. The possibilities are endless and depend on the setup. For example, if you wish to create two instances, one of which has to be completely finished before the next one is created, it would be best to have a CloudFormation template which creates the first instance and outputs the information needed by another template for its creation. With this stacking method, you can create complex systems with creation dependencies met. An example of an outputs section might resemble:

```
"Outputs": {
  "WebServerELB": {
    "Description": "The A record of the ELB for the web instance.",
    "Value": {
      "Fn::GetAtt": ["WebServerELB", "DNSName"]
    }
  }
}
```

With that short description in mind, let's get started. From the CloudFormation dashboard, select **Create Stack**.

From the **Select Template** window, create a name for our stack `test-Stack`, upload the template included with the book, and select **Next**.

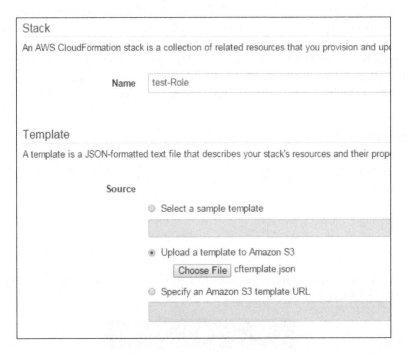

Since our template has parameters, you will come to a screen **Specify Parameters**. Specify any parameters relevant to your environment and select **Next**.

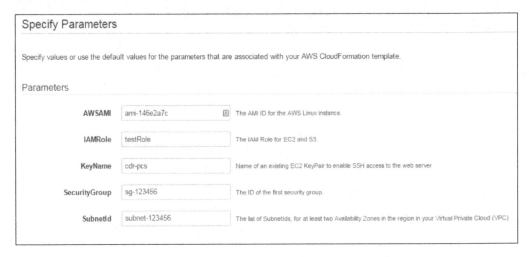

There are no changes to be made from the **Options** page so go ahead and click **Next**. From here we can finish the creation by clicking **Create** from the **Review** page. The creation will now begin and will take some time to complete. You can view its progress from the CloudFormation dashboard.

Once the stack is finished, **Status** will change from **CREATE_IN_PROGRESS** to **CREATE_COMPLETE**.

From here, we can verify that everything works as expected by clicking **test-Stack** from the list and selecting the **Outputs** tab.

To do the final verification, copy **Value** for **Web server** and browse to that via a web browser:

We have now completely deployed a stack that consists of a database, load balancer, and web frontend with very little effort. This process could be streamlined using the APIs provided via AWS as well. We can also destroy all of the resources that were created, by simply clicking **Delete Stack** from the CloudFormation console. This completes the stack deployment pattern.

Monitoring integration pattern

One of the many great things about the AWS ecosystem is the amount of tooling at your disposal. A very large portion of work for any operations team is the monitoring of the systems' health. These checks could be scratch-level checks such as CPU usage, RAM information, and disk information. However, monitoring applications is not an easy task.

When it comes to knowing whether or not a system is actually performing, it is more than just knowing if the hardware is fine: it's about knowing a slew of other information that changes based on the perspective of the operations team as well as the architecture of the application itself.

If it is a Java application, is the JVM configured and running as expected? If it's a PHP application, does the system have enough memory allocated to the engine? There are some questions that are fuzzy in nature. For example, if it's a database, are there any queries that are taking 'too long'?

The good thing is that AWS has created the CloudWatch service to answer some of these questions and provide the ability to answer the others. We have discussed CloudWatch in some detail in previous patterns, but the point I am trying to drive home is that this service is likely not enough for most teams. By default, CloudWatch only records information for two weeks. For most teams and applications, this might be completely satisfactory, but for some it may not be.

To see trends over time, two weeks may not be enough time to scan these metrics and come up with solid patterns. In some cases, it may be enough to archive this information.

Many well written pieces of software are available to solve this problem, such as Nagios, Zabbix, Cacti, and others. There is no right answer, so this pattern only attempts to drive home the idea, not the execution.

A lot can be gained by integrating these metrics, application or system logs, or as much information as is possible, into a central repository. They could be retained for contractual reasons, security audits, pattern observations, deep health checks; the possibilities are endless. A lot of care should be taken when choosing the right central store as it is usually difficult, generally expensive, and time consuming to reverse this process and move it from one repository to another.

Web storage archive pattern

The next pattern will aim at a smaller subset of archival as compared to the previous monitoring integration pattern. While the previous pattern was a more theoretical approach to the larger aggregation and archival schema, sometimes it is relevant to only archive certain files. One choice might be to dump the database to the filesystem. This may not be the best choice for all use cases but it is still a common approach.

A much more common practice is to rotate files, such as logs, out of the server and into a permanent store as they grow over time. There are plenty of ways to do this, such as remote syslog, or some log services such as Loggly or Logstash. It is such a common practice that there are literally hundreds of third-party solutions to choose from.

To demonstrate this, we will use logrotate which is included in nearly every major Linux distribution. Logrotate will handle the file rotation, compression, and synchronization with Amazon S3. The configuration also includes timing, naming scheme, as well as many other small tweaks for the rotation itself.

For our configuration, we will make use of a `postrotate` directive, which will allow us to sync the log directory to our previously created `1ce8b98d-8735-47ff-a9dc-7f4b57820a74` bucket.

First, launch an AWS instance from the AWS Linux AMI as we have many times from the EC2 console. Note that since we are going to sync our logs into S3, we must use **IAM role** `testRole` that we created in the previous patterns. Once it is ready, SSH into it.

Create a file `/etc/logrotate.d/myapp` with the contents:

```
compress
compresscmd /bin/gzip
compressoptions -9
compressext .gz

dateext
dateformat -%Y-%m-%d-%s

rotate 2
nomail
missingok
size 1k

/var/log/test/*.log {
sharedscripts
postrotate
aws s3 sync /var/log/test/ s3://1ce8b98d-8735-47ff-a9dc-7f4b57820a74/
--exclude "*" --include "*.gz"
endscript
}
EOF
```

Before we go any further, let us break down the configuration file a bit.

The first section, as shown in the following code, defines the compression. We will use the `gzip` utility on the file and give it some compression metadata.

```
compress
compresscmd /bin/gzip
compressoptions -9
compressext .gz
```

The next section defines the naming and rotation scheme. We will give it a naming scheme that is time stamped to make it readable and sortable automatically. We will also specify that it is ok if there are no files to compress, as well as set the minimum size to rotate of 1K (1 kilobyte). Lastly, we will set it to rotate 2, or keep only the two latest compressed files.

```
dateext
dateformat -%Y-%m-%d-%s
rotate 2
missingok
size 1k
```

The last section is the most important part and actually defines our rotation process. We need to tell logrotate where the logs live and what their file extension is, in this case .log. With the sharedscripts directive, we are telling logrotate to only run the postrotate processor once, even if multiple files were rotated. Lastly, we have given a postrotate block that is the S3 CLI command, to sync the files with S3. In the current CLI usage, however, in order to specify only a certain file type to sync (.gz), we must first exclude all files. This prevents us from syncing the log file itself, or the uncompressed files that are in the compression process.

```
/var/log/test/*.log {
sharedscripts
postrotate
aws s3 sync /var/log/test/ s3://1ce8b98d-8735-47ff-a9dc-7f4b57820a74/
--exclude "*" --include "*.gz"
endscript
}
```

Now that the configuration file exists, we will create a CRON (or timer) entry that runs logrotate every minute. Modify the /etc/crontab file and add the following line to the bottom:

```
*/1 * * * * root logrotate --state /var/run/log_rotate.state /etc/
logrotate.d/myapp >>/var/log/logrotate 2>&1
```

Lastly, let's create a log file and watch it get rotated. Run the following commands to do this. Please note that these commands, by virtue of the sleep commands, will take around five minutes to complete:

```
mkdir /var/log/test
for i in {1..4}; do for j in {1..100}; do  uuidgen >>/var/log/test/stuff.
log; done; sleep 75; done
```

Once complete, we can verify that only two compressed files exist in our `/var/log/test` directory:

```
[ec2-user@ip-10-203-10-109 ~]$ sudo ls -alh /var/log/test
total 16K
drwxr-xr-x 2 root root 4.0K Feb 13 03:52 .
drwxr-xr-x 6 root root 4.0K Feb 13 03:48 ..
-rw-r--r-- 1 root root 2.1K Feb 13 03:51 stuff.log-2015-02-13-1423799461.
gz
-rw-r--r-- 1 root root 2.1K Feb 13 03:52 stuff.log-2015-02-13-1423799521.
gz
```

But more importantly, let us verify that all the other logs have been synchronized to our S3 bucket:

This concludes the web storage archive pattern.

Weighted transition pattern

The previous patterns, up until this point, either help to mitigate encountered problems or give unique solutions to possible problems. We have not discussed a lot of patterns that help to test our infrastructure.

Perhaps our system consists of a web server and a database server, as is often the case. Upgrading these can be done incrementally with zero downtime, as we've shown in previous patterns, but we have only discussed ways to do a full upgrade.

Let us suppose that some code changes are pending deployment on the web instance that requires a migration on the database instance. This is a hefty change that might cause a lot of headaches if it is not tested thoroughly before being released into a production environment. While testing it in a staging system is quite common and is a great way to uncover issues, both from usage and from a deployment standpoint, it may not catch everything.

The weighted transition pattern is one of the many patterns that exist for this reason. In this pattern, the new infrastructure is deployed alongside the previous infrastructure, so that both the old instances as well as the new instances are running side by side. From here we use a DNS weighting of which we set the **Route53** entry for our new instance to receive a low portion of the traffic.

Combining this pattern with something similar to the previous monitoring integration pattern will allow the operations team to see if the new system is performing as expected. A set up might resemble:

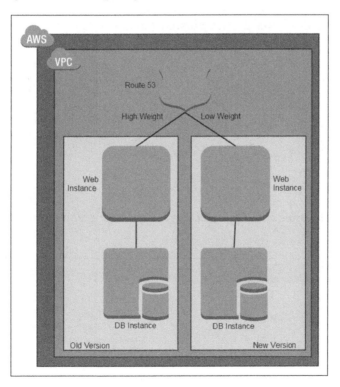

For this pattern, we will not cover the instances themselves but will instead cover how to set up weighted DNS entries in **Route53**, and prove that a small amount of traffic would resolve to the new set of instances instead of the old.

It should be noted that if this set up was implemented as-is, then, post deployment, there would be slight data discrepancies in the new instance. Suppose that this set up is left in effect for a long time, or a short time with a lot of traffic. At some point, the databases will diverge in terms of data and might result in some unpleasant side effects to the end users. Traditional ways to resolve this would be to have the new database replicate from the old database, with triggers in place to allow the old unmigrated data to be stored. There is no right answer to this as it depends on the infrastructure at hand, but if the application depends on the state of the data, there might be many issues associated with following this pattern as-is. The fact is, this pattern is designed to test the system and might require a multitude of additional changes if it is to become a deployment pattern.

First browse to the Route53 **Dashboard** in AWS. From here, I will have to assume that a hosted zone already exists for your account, as the process of creating one has a lot of dependencies not relevant to the pattern. Also, if the environment is not already properly configured with a hosted zone, there would be no way to test it.

From the Route53 **Dashboard,** click **Hosted Zones**.

From the **Hosted Zones** console, select any hosted zone you control and click **Go to Record Sets**.

From here, we will create two new **A** records. Click **Create Record Set**.

We will now create the record set. Set the values as shown in the following screen shot, being sure to change the **Routing Policy** value in the drop down to **Weighted,** and finish the creation by selecting **Create**.

Repeat the process, one more time, by creating an A record for a different **Value** and a higher **Weight**.

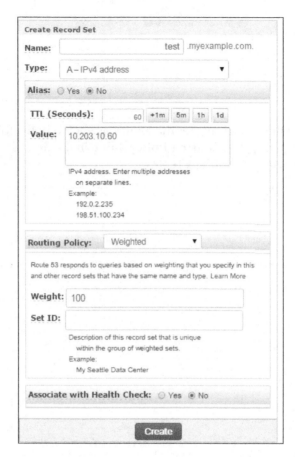

What we have done at this point is create multiple **A** records that Route53 will alternate by round robin weighting. The record for `10.203.10.50` has a lower weight of `10` while the other record of `10.203.10.60` has a higher weight of `100`. If we were to try to resolve the record `test.myexample.com` multiple times, we would resolve it to the higher weight IP address more often. So let us prove this. Create a file with the following contents from any computer that can run bash such as Linux, Mac OS X, or even Cygwin for Windows:

```
#!/bin/bash
low_weight=0
high_weight=0

for i in {1..50}; do
  result=$(dig test.myexample.com +short)
```

```
    [[ "${result}" == "10.203.10.50" ]] && low_weight=$[$low_weight +1]
|| high_weight=$[$high_weight +1]
done

echo "low weight: ${low_weight}"
echo "high weight: ${high_weight}"
Running that script yields:
low weight: 6
high weight: 44
```

This proves that Route53 routed our traffic 44 times out of 50 to the instance with the higher weight. This means that 12% of our traffic would have gone to the new instance if it were configured correctly. This concludes the weighted transition pattern.

Hybrid backup pattern

Previously, we have covered a few patterns that discuss how to back up using Amazon provided services, but those patterns assumed that all assets were in Amazon. In real-world situations, it is very rare that all of a team's assets are in a single store such as Amazon.

These transitional and hybrid data centre setups are quite common, but a lot of management headaches come with trying to secure backups on-site. A solution to this that helps to ease the transition and even to ease some backup issues such as continuity and redundancy, is to use a hybrid backup pattern.

This pattern will not be covered in-depth as it is impossible to cover all the edge cases for types of backups as well as ways to ship the data into AWS. One of the easiest ways to put backups into S3 is by using some of the previous patterns in which we copied data to S3, as that access is transparent. However, S3 is not the only solution. Amazon Glacier is a bit cheaper but is considered cold storage.

Uploading and downloading from S3 is near to real-time, excluding some specified time required to replicate the data. However, Glacier is not real-time. Uploading and downloading orders of magnitude from the Glacier service might take longer than S3, so it should be noted that the choice depends on how readily available the data needs to be.

 More information on the Glacier service can be found on the documentation page at http://aws.amazon.com/glacier/.

Summary

In this chapter, we elaborated on previous patterns, such as those in *Chapter 2, Basic Patterns*, to come up with some practical and theoretical solutions to issues and deployment concerns. In the bootstrap pattern, we discussed how to separate the actual data from the user data of the instance, so that small tweaks to our web application could be made quickly and with few downstream effects. We then moved to the Cloud dependency injection pattern in which we showed how to separate the user data completely from the instance using information from the tags provided via the API, then injecting them at boot-time. Next, we covered the stack deployment pattern, in which we covered in some detail how to launch an entire stack, or in our case a web application and a database, in a single transaction. This allowed us to quickly deploy with little room for error. We next covered the monitoring integration pattern, in which we discussed some of the issues with the CloudWatch service, and how we can use third party software to create a central store for metrics and other information that might be lost over time. Continuing on this concept, we covered the web storage archive pattern and showed how to use the Linux logrotate utility to move logs into S3, saving disk space and future headaches caused by missing logs. Next, we touched on the theoretical concept of using Route53 to allow a small amount of traffic to an alternate stack of software, so that we might monitor how an upgrade would affect the overall system. Finally, in the hybrid backup pattern, we discussed how one might use Amazon services to allow on-site machines to back up outside of their data centre, possibly saving money and time.

In the next chapter, we will continue on the operational path and discuss patterns for networking.

10
Patterns for Networking

Many of the patterns, or arguably almost all, discussed in this book cover patterns for the virtual machines themselves: from ensuring that data exists across machines to ensuring that there are no single points of failure.

In the previous chapter, we covered a bit more from the infrastructure side of moving to the Cloud such as integrating logs in the monitoring integration pattern to discussing how one might use AWS to host backups from an on-premises set of machines. Continuing on this path, we will move much more heavily into infrastructure theory in this chapter.

The patterns we will discuss, in order, are:

- OnDemand NAT pattern: This allows the entire subnets of machines to have internet access as-needed.
- Management network pattern: This uses multiple network adapters to route specific traffic.
- Functional firewall pattern: This uses firewall rules for individual machines by a specific functionality.
- Operational firewall pattern: This groups firewall rules for specific services or organizations.
- Web application firewall pattern: This uses application-specific firewalls to safeguard against behavior.
- Multiple load-balancer pattern: This uses load balancers to terminate outside connections.

OnDemand NAT pattern

It should be noted that the issue of security is not the topic of this book. We will not discuss how to secure the systems overall, but we will touch lightly on some concerns and how it is possible to use Amazon-provided services or configurations to start the movement into that world.

With that said we will use the following example: suppose the instances we wish to bring up do not have internet access but still need to talk to other instances. This could be for security—as it prevents outside access to our instances and adds a layer of hardening—or for simplicity. This is very relevant in the microservices architecture if it can be architected in such a way that outside connectivity is not needed.

To do this, we can use a **Network Address Translation (NAT)** instance in our environment to our advantage. We can set up our normal instances to send their non-local traffic to this NAT instance. By doing this, we can effectively turn on and off access to the outside internet by simply disabling the interface when needed or even shutting off the entire instance. The latter might be preferred as it saves on billing costs since instances that are not active accrue no charges.

If maintenance on our instances is needed, such as security or package updates, we can simply re-enable the interface or turn on the instance. This will allow us to maintain a set of systems that cannot be penetrated by normal means from the outside world. In theory, the only way these instances could be compromised is if they were able to control a machine within the same subnet or had access to them through a VPN connection.

An example of this type of setup can be seen as follows:

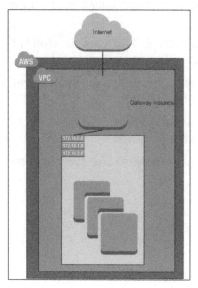

Of course, as with all patterns, there are some downsides to consider. Firstly, this operates on the assumption that the instances can work without access to the internet, which seems to be a rare condition in most machines. The bigger downside, however, is that with this pattern there is no way to use AWS-provided services such as S3 while the interface or instance is down. Traffic from VPC into S3 traverses the public domain. This is also true for many other services and configurations such as elastic load balancers. Take caution when implementing this pattern.

Management network pattern

Continuing from the previous pattern of managing the network traffic by way of routing, we will move to managing the traffic through distinct interfaces. As with physical machines it is possible to have multiple network interfaces.

In the previous pattern, the machine relied on a single interface for all traffic in and out. We might extend on this instead of having two interfaces: one to be responsible for all the traffic to and from the outside internet and the other would be responsible for the traffic to an on-site data center. This alternate network traffic is sometimes referred to as a backnet or management network.

By creating our interfaces in this fashion there is a clear distinction of responsibilities and separation of concerns. Also, this makes it much easier to apply AWS-provided firewall configurations or Security Groups. Security Groups are provided as a first-class AWS configuration that acts as firewall rules to other AWS entities such as EC2 instances. Security Groups can be stand-alone rules or may be stacked.

More information for Security Groups can be found on the AWS documentation page available at http://docs.aws.amazon.com/ AWSEC2/latest/UserGuide/using-network-security.html.

The real benefit of Security Groups to this pattern is that they are tied directly to the network interfaces themselves. By having multiple interfaces, we can easily manage generic firewall rules for the management network and have a very specific and open rule for the interface that faces the internet. A simple visual representation can be found in the following diagram:

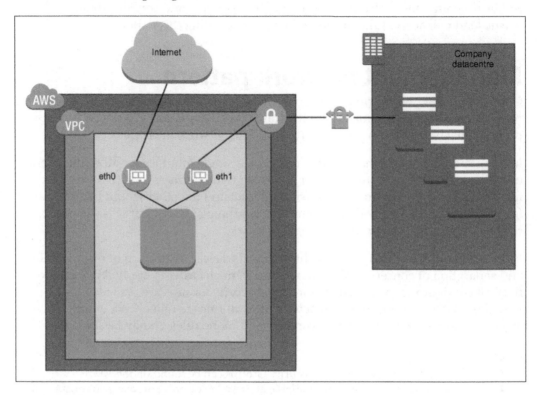

A big benefit of this pattern is that it allows you to migrate some infrastructure to the Cloud in a way that lets it operate in tandem with alternate services provided by the company. This is a good way to shift to the Cloud without having to move all the infrastructure in one single pass. It also sets the stage for a hybrid infrastructure so that companies can use their existing infrastructure with little interruption.

 A note to be made, however, is that since the traffic travels over a VPN connection from the **VPC** in the preceding diagram, the cost might be more as all the traffic that is not going out to the internet travels over the secure line.

Functional firewall pattern

A lot of security concerns are not from the software themselves, but from the configuration surrounding the infrastructure. For example, consider a setup that has dozens or hundreds of instances, each with their own internal firewall configurations. Without the use of the configuration management software such as Puppet or Chef or a very fine process regarding this configuration, each instance may end up with a slightly different set of rules from the next.

Add to this example that the infrastructure itself may have similar configuration such as the AWS-provided Security Groups. With these many instances, it could get out of control very quickly if care is not taken from the beginning or is iterated over repeatedly. Some groups may conflict with others, cause gaps in protection, or just not work as expected. What started as a good process might evolve into a spider web of headaches.

One benefit of Security Groups is their flexibility: they can be stacked on top of each other, reference other Security Groups, and be granular or broad in scope. In the functional firewall pattern we will demonstrate the benefit of grouping Security Groups and referencing other Security Groups to create an easy-to-manage and simple-to-understand setup.

Consider the following diagram:

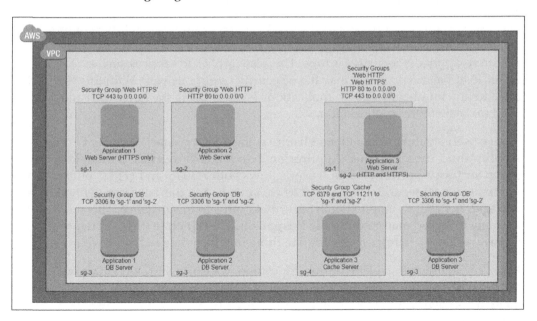

In this figure, we have defined three entirely different applications, creatively named **Application 1**, **Application 2**, and **Application 3**. All of these are web server applications that have a database and possible cache server such as MemCached or Redis. If we follow the original example, we might end up with as many as seven firewall configurations (one per instance).

A change to one will not affect the others, which allows for the possibility of an error if this change is needed in all similar applications such as changing the default database port. Instead, we have defined only four Security Groups:

- sg-1: This is responsible for allowing HTTPS (port 443) from any source such as internet users. It would also allow other instances in the AWS account to talk to it.

- sg-2: This is responsible for default HTTP traffic (port 80) from any source similar to sg-1.

- sg-3: This is responsible for default database traffic (MySQL default TCP port 3306) from anything in the sg-1 or sg-2 Security Groups. These will not allow traffic from external sources such as internet users or even anything in the AWS account not mentioned in the Security Groups.

- sg-4: This is responsible for default cache server traffic (Redis default port 6379 and MemCached default port 11211) from anything in the sg-1 or sg-2 Security Groups similar to sg-3.

This configuration is very easy to read and extend. From a readability standpoint, it means that if we add any new applications or even scale out any current instances, we can re-apply the Security Groups. This also applies to services such as AWS elastic load balancers, which may have Security Groups as well. With this setup, we can add any number of similar applications (similar being the key word) and will not need to create more configuration.

A very useful feature as mentioned before is the ability to stack Security Groups. **Application 1** uses SSL while **Application 2** does not so we created a single security group for this. **Application 3**, however, allows both HTTPS and HTTP, but we did not create a new security group for it as we already had this behavior defined in **sg-1** and **sg-2**. Instead, we applied both Security Groups to this instance. This follows a widely followed mantra of **Single Responsibility Principle (SRP)** in which our Security Groups are responsible for one thing in which they will do it well.

By following this principle in our configuration, we can easily extend this out further without compromising the integrity of our policies and adding artifacts or edge cases, such as accidentally allowing internet users to create a connection to the database or cache instances.

Operational firewall pattern

Continuing from the previous example, it may not be enough to just group your servers by function. The previous example would work great for general web pages that are accessible to the public, but would not work well if the applications needed to be controlled are on a per-client or per-system basis.

Refer to the following diagram:

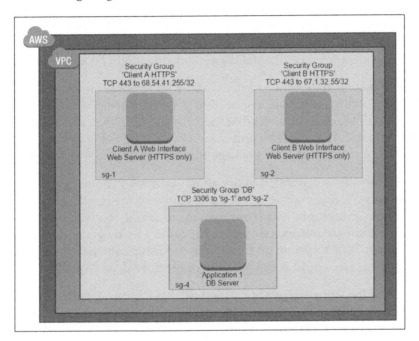

This diagram looks very similar to the previous one, except we have simplified it down to a single application with separate front-end instances. The database instance still contains a security group that allows anything in the web interfaces (**sg-1** and **sg-2**) while the web interfaces are bound to an organization (the client).

In the previous functional firewall pattern, these web interfaces would have the same Security Group; however, by binding them to an organization (such as a consuming system or client), we can easily change what is relevant to that organization without affecting the others. This might include managing a client-specific certificate, the source IP, and so on. It also very easily allows a system administrator to know which instances are for what purposes and who it affects.

While this does have some benefits to security, the biggest benefit to these is the ability to reduce errors or add unnecessary side effects to the system in an area that might be hard to troubleshoot.

Web application firewall pattern

The next pattern is not specific to the Cloud, but is important enough to mention. When securing a system it is one thing to prevent or limit access, but that is only a small scope of a much broader assessment. Suppose your database does not allow connection from anything other than the web instance that is connected to it.

While this means that no outside system can directly access the instance, it does not mean that they cannot compromise it and change that assertion. A traditional firewall or even Security Groups will never prevent behavior from individuals such as SQL injection and exploiting bugs in software. While the system administrators had a firewall rule in place of the database, someone might be able to modify that.

That is where intrusion detection systems and web application firewalls come into play. We will not discuss intrusion detection systems, but since we are on the topic of firewalls, we will touch lightly on what they are and how they can be implemented in a Cloud infrastructure. A web application firewall can come in many forms: from a SaaS appliance or an installable package to just a set of configuration files.

A traditional firewall is stateful: it either allows or denies connections. An application firewall, however, inspects the behavior of the application. Let's refer to our previous examples in which our system consisted of a web instance running Apache and a database instance that it could connect to. By general use, this is fine, but if we were to base a system on the simple code snippets that were provided in previous chapters, we could very likely be compromised very quickly.

For example, in the snippets, our SQL queries from *Chapter 6, Patterns for Uploading Data* were never sanitized, had no error handling, and could likely cause one or both of the systems to be compromised from a malicious user via SQL injection or many other common penetration methods. The firewall would never prevent it as its job is simply to allow or deny the user access. However, using a web application firewall such as ModSecurity would help to find this behavior and prevent it or at the very least detect it.

[More information on ModSecurity can be found at https://www.modsecurity.org/.]

However, thinking about this from a Cloud perspective, things get a bit difficult. For example, software that adheres to PCI compliance (dealing with credit card information) has strict rules for what it means to be in compliance and how to deal with data breaches. While there are free application firewalls that could be mixed and matched to meet these requirements, the company may opt for a non-free version, which is the more common case.

The licensing for this software most likely is on a per-instance basis and thinking back to our patterns that is the opposite of what we are usually trying to achieve with a dynamic Cloud infrastructure. The ability to scale out as needed or failover as soon as possible might not work with a set licensing requirement. In times like these, the system might be architected in such a way that the firewall does not live side by side with the instances being protected.

By moving the application firewall out of the instances, we are able to scale out the instances themselves with no concern to licensing, but we are also able to know how many licenses are in use or are required ahead of time. For a visual representation, refer to the following diagram:

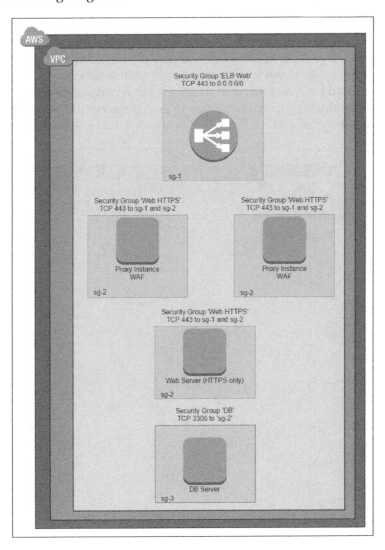

In this example, what we have done is carefully defined how many web application firewall instances we have at any given time, making licensing easy (although at the cost of not being able to autoscale). We are still able to scale out the web instances without worrying about the firewalls, although registering with the proxy would be the next step to take care of. Lastly, if we look carefully, we have tied in our original functional firewall pattern in that there are only three Security Groups to manage.

Multiple load balancer pattern

The last firewall pattern we will discuss will be an elaboration on the operational firewall pattern. If we look back at this pattern, we will see that we not only grouped the instances by function, but also by what outside operation or customer it was relevant to. This might work if we had client-specific web pages, but that is rarely the case when it comes to an application. It might also be noted that if we terminate SSL somewhere else, upstream it saves some computation time (arguably low). AWS-provided load balancers allow us to specify the certificate information thereby allowing us to terminate the SSL connection in an AWS service, potentially saving us some computation cycles and configuration headaches. Refer to the following diagram:

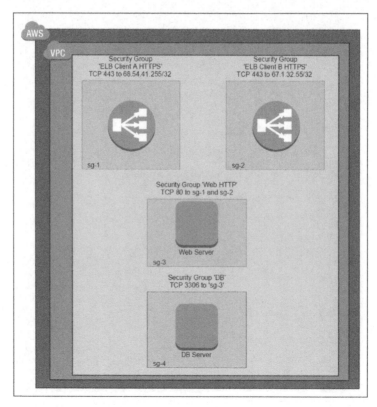

In this example, we have a single web instance that communicates over native HTTP (port 80) and allows connections from the load balancers (which have client, customer, or organization-specific Security Groups: **sg-1** and **sg-2**). With this method, we no longer have to manage multiple certificates in a single instance or even certificate information per client in our instances at all, but operate under normal HTTP traffic. The load balancers here will do the heavy lifting of allowing or rejecting the traffic and deciding whether the certificate is valid.

We can now scale out our web instances through any combination of the patterns discussed in this book and we will not even have to worry about the Security Groups as we have only one for the web instance (**sg-3**). This also holds true for the database instances since there is only one security group (**sg-4**) so we can scale out through any of the previous database patterns. We can also make use of the AWS that provides RDS databases as we can apply our Security Groups there as well.

Summary

In this chapter, we continued from *Chapter 9, Patterns for Operation and Maintenance* and stayed in the realm of the underlying infrastructure: networks. In the OnDemand NAT pattern, we discussed how to effectively turn on and off outside connectivity so that we can prevent unwanted access except when maintenance windows are needed. We then moved to the management network pattern in which we discussed how to route traffic over the interfaces themselves within a virtual machine so that we can easily distinguish outside traffic from other AWS traffic, or even traffic from an on-premises data center. Next, we covered the functional firewall pattern in which we showed how we can use the AWS-provided firewall configuration (Security Groups) to group instances by their functional part in a stack. Staying on the firewall topic, we discussed how to group virtual machines, not only by their function in the stack, but also by who the clients are. Finishing up the firewall discussions, we ended with web application firewalls and how we can protect our system from the behavior of the clients and users instead of only relying on allowing or disallowing traffic overall. The last pattern is the multiple load balancer pattern in which we discussed how to move the certificate configuration and firewall management for outside systems that are completely out of our hands and into the AWS-managed elastic load balancers: saving us time and computation.

We will finish this book with the next chapter in which we talk in theory about how to use new third-party technologies with AWS to create systems that can be recreated as often as possible. This next chapter will also describe the current trend of blurring the DevOps line and move developers closer to the deployment process.

11
Throw-away Environments

Throughout this book, we covered many patterns that can be applied to scenarios, but are flexible in many ways. They can be mixed and matched, even stacked to create very cool setups. This is only one piece of the much larger puzzle, however, of getting into the Cloud mindset.

My assumption for this book is that you, the reader, have already moved many resources out into the AWS infrastructure. One thing we have not discussed is how to continue after the migration is complete. Perhaps the application was shifted there, and it is now running perfectly and can mend itself when problems are encountered.

From here, though, the questions shift to a whole different set of problems and issues. Perhaps the application consists of a web page and database. How do you deploy it out there? Do you take an approach similar to the previous chapters in which we hosted straight from S3? If so, how do you handle code changes that require database changes? If we push that code directly into S3 or whatever underlying service without staging the database changes, it could cause some problems to the end user. Even further, what if the database migration fails or just takes an obscene amount of time to complete in production?

The point of these questions is to hint at the overall optimization of moving the developers closer to the final product. If the point of these chapters was to prevent the downtime and create resilient applications, then we have missed a big section: the underlying pieces.

Say, for instance, we have an application that is spread across two availability zones. We have designed it to be fault-tolerant and resilient, but a disaster happens: an entire availability zone is gone or inaccessible; or perhaps we did all of this work in availability zones in Virginia, but a new data center is created and becomes available much closer to you.

Would the move be easy? Perhaps it is, but perhaps it's not: our examples had some hard-coded `export AWS_DEFAULT_REGION=us-east-1a` in many places, which would be simple to miss. Also, do not forget to calculate in the amount of time it would take to bring up VPC, create subnets, enable VPN connections, and create the gateway instance we rely on. We will touch on a few topics in this chapter:

- Infrastructure as a code: This puts the traditional development practices on the hardware abstractions.

- Temporary development environments: This moves the developers closer to the final servers to prevent inconsistency as early as possible.

- Continuous integration: This optimizes our deployment and testing practices to get a bit more power from Cloud infrastructure.

Infrastructure as code

Many development shops have a very big mantra for quality control surrounding code. What gets missed from the operations or DevOps teams is very similar in terms of requiring quality control over the infrastructure. The movement lately is to be ensured that the infrastructure is treated the same as the code itself. By putting the same practices in place; it is easy to view, control, and replicate these environments. For example, if security groups are modified, then it is easy to track down what caused the change.

This enables us to do audits as well. If something were to open up ports to a server or security group configuration, we would know fairly quickly whether it was done by accident or through malicious intent. This also means that if our infrastructure needed to shift to a new region or availability zone, or if the hardware underneath our infrastructure experiences a catastrophic failure, we can recover somewhat easily.

CloudFormation

We actually have touched slightly on this topic through our stack deployment pattern from *Chapter 9, Patterns for Operation and Maintenance*, using CloudFormation templates. CloudFormation, as we stated, can manage nearly anything that exists in AWS. This includes subnets, routing tables, DHCP option sets, and all the pieces that can actually determine our entire infrastructure; not just the virtual machines themselves.

The benefit of CloudFormation to this topic is that once a template is uploaded, it can be updated. Say, for instance, all of our security groups were created through a template. If we needed to have a new IP address for a client or modify an existing one, we could make that change to our template and push it through the normal peer review channels such as code review. After all the changes are approved, it would be applied as an update to the current template and would make the necessary changes.

Packer

HashiCorp has made quite a run at this with their software Packer. Packer is quite different from CloudFormation from the very beginning as it is agnostic to the provider (in this case AWS). It is written on top of components:

- Builders: This is a type of package to create. For this book's examples it would be an AMI, however, it can package as many forms such as Docker containers, DigitalOcean Droplets, and so on.

- Provisioners: This is the bootstrappers for configuration. This could be Shell, Puppet, Chef, Salt, and many others.

- Post-processors: Optional post-processing steps that might be needed such as compression, file upload, and so on.

Packer seems to have a much lower barrier to entry for some, although it is pure preference. CloudFormation, while native, is very verbose in its textual representation and lacks the ability to output to other formats or Cloud providers.

> More information about Packer can be found on their webpage at www.packer.io.

Fugue

Another choice to create infrastructure from code is Fugue. Fugue is a start-up currently based in Washington, DC that aims at automating and controlling infrastructure, from the hardware itself to the instances making up the stack.

The configuration files are written in YAML and are aimed directly at AWS infrastructure. At the current state of this chapter, the company is still getting ready to launch their initial beta.

> More information about Fugue can be found on their webpage at www.fugue.it.

Temporary development environments

It is very rare to encounter a stack of software that work together in perfect harmony to a developer. Many developers have to rely on development boxes to do some pieces of their development tasks such as database testing, using cache servers, and so on.

There has been a lot of effort put forth to minimize this, thanks to the software such as Vagrant. I mentioned Vagrant early on, in which we demonstrated how to bootstrap an AWS EC2 instance from a configuration file. The real power to it, however, is bringing the developers closer to the environment that it will be deployed under.

For example, imagine a team that works on a Ruby on Rails application. Each developer uses a Macintosh since it can handle Ruby natively. Many developers, however, may use different versions of Ruby and write their code that way. During deployment, this is not communicated and the code is shipped out onto a CentOS box, which uses a much older version of Ruby. The code has a high likelihood of being incompatible.

This could have been prevented in many ways before deployment using continuous integration suites such as TeamCity, Jenkins, or even Bamboo and it would be a nightmare to discover too late. Another common mishap is that a developer may use third-party plugins that do not make their way to the final production server or rely on system level calls that may not even be available.

Using something like Vagrant, we could enable our developers to work locally on development machines that target and mimic the production environment almost exactly. This practice has been extremely practical in my run of blurring the lines between a developer and operations. I have personally found it extremely helpful to allow developers to know the limitations and details of the production server. It has allowed them to write robust code that can be modified easily from an operation's perspective.

For example, if the developers know how AWS user data works when writing a new system application, they can, from the very beginning, avoid pitfalls of attempting to hardcode things that should not be hardcoded such as certificate locations, database connection strings, configuration options, and so on. This makes the handoff to a staging ground almost seamless.

Lastly, it makes the barrier to entry much lower for the new members of the team. A large amount of time is spent by a developer in the first few weeks with a team trying to get their computers or laptops prepared. Instead of requiring them to try to memorize where the development servers are, what versions of software they are running, how to interact with them, and so on, these configuration files explain nearly everything at a glance.

Their first week could be much better spent by allowing them to just work by bringing up the servers they need as they need them.

The most important benefit to take from temporary environments is the ability to test as early as possible how a deployment or set of changes would affect the application overall. Every time a machine is created from Vagrant, it is at the same place in terms of configuration. If a database migration is needed, it cannot be missed as this latest machine that was brought up does not have it. This means that we are constantly testing our underlying pieces.

Continuous integration

The traditional **continuous integration** (CI) is another gray area for developers. CI servers typically consist of a master and slave setup. The master(s) controls the builds, or how to run the tests or commands, and the slaves execute them.

The fantastic thing about Cloud infrastructure, as we have discussed many times, is the ability to spin up instances as needed and terminate them when we are done with them. This gives us a very unique opportunity: ad-hoc CI slaves.

Using Cloud infrastructure we most likely should have the master running 24/7. This prevents us from having gaps in commits. If there are no agents available, the builds will stay in a queue of some sort. The agents, however, can be Cloud agents and spun up as needed.

Perhaps we deploy an application that can be installed on both CentOS and Ubuntu platforms. From the master, we could have a build configuration that uses a pre-built AMI for both of these operating systems so that we can test and build on each without constantly having both running.

It would be pretty wasteful on resources, for example, to have 20 agents that are not doing anything, especially so on weekends and holidays. From an AWS perspective, this means there are many hours that are being billed, which we are not making use of.

Summary

In this final chapter, we discussed some high-level topics that are making headlines in the DevOps movement and can heavily improve our work with AWS infrastructure. Firstly, we talked about how to move our infrastructure into a code. This allows us to apply things such as peer review, diffing tools, and so on against pending changes to our infrastructure. Next, we moved to temporary development environments and discussed how tools such as Vagrant allow us to get the final servers much closer to the developers. This can prevent things such as software incompatibilities, miscommunications about migrations, and a slew of other possible errors when it is time to get our code to the consuming clients. Finally, we discussed how we can optimize our testing and deployment to make use of the flexibility of the Cloud and AWS. This concludes this book.

Index

K

Key Value Store (KVS) 90

L

log-gathering 9
Logical Unit Number (LUN) 12
logs
  monitoring 9

M

management network pattern 187, 188
MemCached
  URL 90
ModSecurity
  about 192
  URL 192
monitoring integration pattern 174
multi-data center pattern 48, 49
multiple load balancer pattern 194, 195
multi-server pattern
  about 42
  workflow 42-48
MySQL Fabric
  about 121, 128
  URL 121

N

Network Address Translation (NAT) 186
Network File Sharing (NFS) pattern 85-89
networking
  functional firewall pattern 189, 190
  management network pattern 187, 188
  multiple load balancer pattern 194, 195
  OnDemand NAT pattern 186, 187
  operational firewall pattern 191
  web application firewall pattern 192-194

O

on-demand disk pattern
  about 32, 33
  I/O, increasing through
      software RAID 36-38

volume, changing from magnetic to SSD 36
volume, resizing 34
OnDemand NAT pattern 186, 187
operational firewall pattern 191
over-provisioning 7

P

Packer
  about 199
  URL 199
Platform as a Service (PaaS) 4
priority queue pattern 142-148
private data delivery 70-72

Q

queuing chain pattern 135-141

R

read replica pattern 121, 122
Redis
  URL 90
Redis ruby client
  URL 93
redundancy 8
Relational Database Service (RDS) 2
rename distribution pattern 76
replication 8
Route53 179

S

scale out pattern
  about 23
  process 23-31
scale up pattern 19-22
Security Groups
  about 187
  reference link 187
  sg-1 190
  sg-2 190
  sg-3 190
  sg-4 190
security policies
  references 62

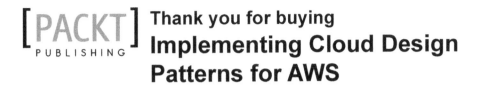

Thank you for buying
Implementing Cloud Design Patterns for AWS

About Packt Publishing

Packt, pronounced 'packed', published its first book, *Mastering phpMyAdmin for Effective MySQL Management*, in April 2004, and subsequently continued to specialize in publishing highly focused books on specific technologies and solutions.

Our books and publications share the experiences of your fellow IT professionals in adapting and customizing today's systems, applications, and frameworks. Our solution-based books give you the knowledge and power to customize the software and technologies you're using to get the job done. Packt books are more specific and less general than the IT books you have seen in the past. Our unique business model allows us to bring you more focused information, giving you more of what you need to know, and less of what you don't.

Packt is a modern yet unique publishing company that focuses on producing quality, cutting-edge books for communities of developers, administrators, and newbies alike. For more information, please visit our website at www.packtpub.com.

Writing for Packt

We welcome all inquiries from people who are interested in authoring. Book proposals should be sent to author@packtpub.com. If your book idea is still at an early stage and you would like to discuss it first before writing a formal book proposal, then please contact us; one of our commissioning editors will get in touch with you.

We're not just looking for published authors; if you have strong technical skills but no writing experience, our experienced editors can help you develop a writing career, or simply get some additional reward for your expertise.

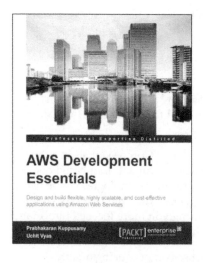

AWS Development Essentials

ISBN: 978-1-78217-361-8   Paperback: 226 pages

Design and build flexible, highly scalable, and cost-effective applications using Amazon Web Services

1. Integrate and use AWS services in an application.

2. Reduce the development time and billing cost using the AWS billing and management console.

3. This is a fast-paced tutorial that will cover application deployment using various tools along with best practices for working with AWS services.

Learning AWS OpsWorks

ISBN: 978-1-78217-110-2   Paperback: 126 pages

Learn how to exploit advanced technologies to deploy and auto-scale web stacks

1. Discover how a DevOps cloud management solution can accelerate your path to delivering highly scalable infrastructure and applications.

2. Learn about infrastructure automation, auto-scaling, and distributed architecture using a Chef-based framework.

3. Includes illustrations, details, and practical examples for successful scaling in the cloud.

Please check **www.PacktPub.com** for information on our titles

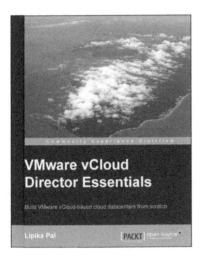

VMware vCloud Director Essentials

ISBN: 978-1-78398-652-1   Paperback: 198 pages

Build VMware vCloud-based cloud datacenters from scratch

1. Learn about DHCP, NAT, and VPN services to successfully implement a private cloud.

2. Configure different networks such as Direct connect, Routed, or Isolated.

3. Configure and manage vCloud Director's access control.

Getting Started with Oracle Public Cloud

ISBN: 978-1-78217-810-1   Paperback: 96 pages

Master the core concepts of Oracle Public Cloud and its services-Java, Database, Transition, Storage, and Messaging

1. Get to grips with the core concepts of Cloud computing and Oracle Public Cloud services.

2. Learn the best practices to be followed while using Oracle Public Cloud.

3. This book will reveal the power of Oracle Public Cloud and show you how you can use this power to your advantage.

Please check **www.PacktPub.com** for information on our titles

Made in the USA
Coppell, TX
16 January 2021